Fly Tying

Other titles in the Crowood Fishing Facts series:

River Trout Fishing   Pat O'Reilly
Stillwater Trout Fishing   Chris Ogborne
Sea Fishing   Trevor Housby
Pike Fishing   Tony Miles
Carp Fishing   Tony Miles

FISHING FACTS

FLY TYING

EXPERT ADVICE FOR BEGINNERS

PAT O'REILLY

Illustrations by Paul Martin

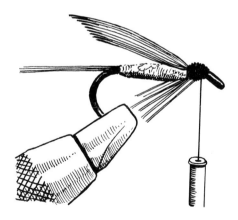

The Crowood Press

First published in 1991 by
The Crowood Press Ltd
Ramsbury, Marlborough
Wiltshire SN8 2HR

British Library Cataloguing in Publication Data

O'Reilly, Pat
Fly tying: expert advice for beginners
1. Angling. Sports equipment
I. Title II. Series
688.7912

ISBN 1 85223 494 6

Typeset by PCS Typesetting, Frome, Somerset.
Printed and bound in Great Britain by
BPCC Hazell Books, Aylesbury

Contents

INTRODUCTION _____

Why Bother?

Soon after taking up fly fishing, most anglers discover the importance of having the right types and sizes of flies. They realize the need for fly patterns to suit conditions which vary tremendously throughout the season. A visit to the tackle shop rarely solves the problem, as most retailers can only afford to stock a limited selection of flies in a restricted range of sizes. If the majority of anglers who visit your local tackle shop fish for rainbow trout in large reservoirs, but you require small dry flies for river trout fishing, the answer may well be 'Sorry, pal...' Frustrating! And should you live in an area where most people fish for salmon, you must expect some disappointments when shopping for stillwater patterns.

Of course, there are times when the same fly pattern, tied in various sizes, will catch salmon, trout and grayling on rivers, streams, lochs and man-made lakes. Be assured, though, that there are many more days when the fish are choosy, insisting on the right pattern and size of fly fished in just the right way. These are the days which sort out the really capable fly fishers from the 'chuck and chance it' brigade.

The majority of competent fly fishers tie their own flies. Some of them would not consider using a fly they had not tied themselves; others with less free time are happy to buy their 'bread-and-butter' flies from a reputable supplier, but they readily turn to their fly-tying vice when a special pattern or size is needed.

There is another good reason why fly fishers should become fly tyers. It is the special satisfaction which comes from deceiving a fish with a fly you have tied yourself. (Perhaps this stems from some primeval instinct – man the hunter, providing food for the family by means of his own skill.) If you are just starting fly tying, I can promise you this experience is something you will greatly enjoy.

About this Book

With the help of this book you should be able with confidence to buy the basic tools and materials necessary for tying flies, and to use them to produce flies for river and stillwater fishing.

If you don't have time to read the book from cover to cover right away, don't worry. It has been written for dipping into at will. There are illustrated topics on the basic principles of tying flies, as well as step-by-step guidance in a range of tying techniques.

As you work through the book you will be shown how to tie successful patterns of nymphs, wet flies, lures and dry flies. These flies have been carefully chosen to introduce a wide range of useful techniques for tails, bodies, wings and hackles. When you reach the end of the book, you will have a valuable selection of flies and some enviable fly-tying skills.

At the back of the book there are names and addresses of fly-tying organizations and material suppliers, a glossary of fly-tying terms, as well as a list of recommended reading to take you further into the realms of advanced fly tying.

Getting Started _____

The Development of River Fly Patterns

There is evidence that fly fishing was being practised around two thousand years ago, but its origin is probably much earlier than that. Certainly many of the earliest references to the sport mention methods of deceiving trout with imitation flies. In the days of Isaac Walton the art was sufficiently advanced for the great man to list several artificial fly patterns. In fact some of the flies we use today have their origins buried in the mists of time. Fortunately, the work of those early fly tyers was handed down through the generations and eventually documented. Indeed, many a present-day trout owes its untimely demise to fly patterns whose inventors will be forever nameless, but immortalized in the patterns they created.

Will he or won't he?

Many of the early flies were fished beneath the surface, with wet-fly fishing techniques being developed to a fine art in Scotland and the north of England. When fly fishing became popular on the clear chalk streams of Hampshire and Wiltshire it was the floating or dry-fly technique which was considered the most sporting method of tempting trout. By the end of the nineteenth century the rule of 'dry fly only' had become deeply entrenched in the south – despite an awareness that the larger river fish rarely feed on the surface.

Evolution of the Artificial Fly

However the dry fly 'purists' were constantly challenged by one G.E.M. Skues, who fished on the River Itchen. Skues made himself unpopular with traditionalists by expounding the virtues of a nymph fished just beneath the surface to represent a hatching fly. Eventually Skues' persuasive arguments won the day, and on most chalk streams it is now permissible to fish either a floating fly or a nymph.

The rot having set in, Frank Sawyer, a Hampshire Avon river-keeper, publicized his 'induced take' method of fishing a heavily weighted nymph from near the river bed. This method of fishing is now widely used by fly fishers on both chalk and rough streams.

The Growth of Stillwater Trout Fishing

Alongside this development of river flies was a growing fund of knowledge of methods of tempting trout from stillwaters. The building of reservoirs for public water supply brought the opportunity for trout fishing to regions whose rivers were unsuitable for the species. Many of these reservoirs are extremely deep, and fishing techniques and lures have been developed to tempt the huge trout which lurk in their depths.

The growing popularity of stillwater trout fishing led many private landowners to excavate small trout pools. Although labelled as 'postage stamp put-and take' fisheries, these small stillwaters make fly fishing accessible to many more people, including disabled people who find river or reservoir fishing too arduous.

Fly-Tying Today

In recent years salmon fishing has undergone a revolution. The complex traditional feather-winged flies are still used, but increasingly anglers are discovering more durable and simple dressings which achieve the same, and possibly better, results.

Getting Started

Fly Tying in Comfort

To enjoy fly tying and to maximize your efficiency you need a well-planned work facility. It need not be large and you certainly don't have to buy a special work bench or storage cupboards, but you must be comfortable and the things you need most often should be conveniently accessible.

You can make a very workable fly-tying facility with just a small table, a chair and some plastic boxes to hold your tools, hooks and tying materials. The table must be sturdy and at a comfortable height for working, but the surface is not of any great consequence because you can always cover it. A large sheet of white card, or better still, blotting paper, will give you a clean working surface. If it gets torn or too dirty, or should you spill your varnish, you can fit a new sheet at very little expense.

Choose a chair which gives you enough back support, and make sure your bench and chair are of the right height to suit your needs. A chair which can be adjusted in height offers a great advantage. I can really recommend those office swivel chairs with adjustable back rests; although they are quite expensive they turn up occasionally in jumble sales and junk shops, so you may be able to pick one up at a bargain price.

If your fly tying will be done in the corner of a room where the lighting is poor, a table lamp may be necessary, otherwise you may suffer from eye strain when trying to tie up tiny dry flies and nymphs. An adjustable lamp, either fixed on the wall or clamped to the edge of your bench, will help you set the direction of illumination just how you want it.

The Storage Problem

You can start fly tying with just a small selection of tools and materials, and I will suggest a suitable starter kit a little later on. Over the years you probably won't add much to your tool kit, but the scope for creativity in fly tying is only limited by your ingenuity and the materials available to you. So it won't be long before you begin collecting and experimenting with a whole host of natural and man-made materials – and as your collection builds up you will need more and more storage space.

Organizing a Fly-Tying Facility

One practical solution is to keep all your tools, and those materials which you use regularly, on or near your fly-tying bench. The materials you need less frequently can then be stored away – perhaps at the back of a cupboard or wardrobe – but they must be in containers sealed against vermin.

Ask your family and friends to save their one- and two-litre plastic ice-cream containers for you; they stack well one above the other and are ideal for storing furs and feathers. It is, however, a good idea to place a mothball in the bottom of each container so that mites and moths are discouraged from entering and causing damage when the lids are off.

Hooks are another essential item whose storage deserves a little thought. Once different types and sizes of hooks get mixed up you can spend a great deal of time sorting through them for just the one you want. Again, waste re-cycling can come to the rescue, for 35mm film canisters are just the right size for storing hooks. A self-adhesive label on each canister can be marked with the manufacturer, hook style and size. If you label the tops of the canisters, you can store them permanently in a spice rack at the back of your bench.

GETTING STARTED

Quality, not Quantity

Many of the most able fly tyers use but a minimum of tools. Indeed, there are a handful of real experts who can tie up just about any pattern of trout or salmon fly whilst holding the hook in one hand and manipulating the materials and threads with the other. For very simple nymph patterns this is not actually all that difficult, but I am not suggesting you make a serious attempt at fly tying without using any tools. What is possible, and from an economic viewpoint very sensible, is to learn to tie flies using a small number of tools. In this way your budget will allow you to buy tools of better quality. High quality tools not only work better when new but, used properly and looked after well, they will last a lifetime. The bare essentials are described below.

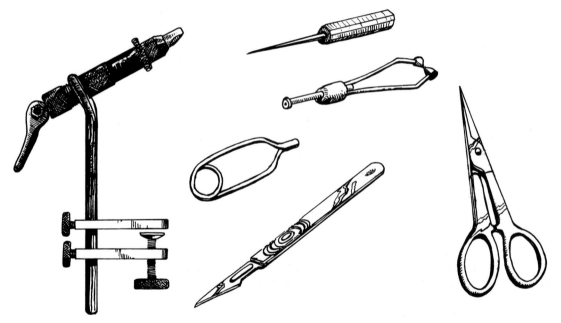

Fly-tying tools.

Vice: Get the best fly-tying vice you can afford. Most fly tyers prefer the lever-operated types which can be rotated without removing the fly from the vice. In any case the vice must have hardened steel jaws capable of holding a hook without it slipping. If possible, test this feature of a vice before making your purchase.

Basic Tools

Bobbin Holders: Strictly speaking a bobbin holder is not an essential item, for you can always cut off the required length of tying thread from the bobbin before you begin tying a fly. The bobbin holder has two great advantages though. First, it greatly reduces the amount of tying thread you will waste, and second it is heavy enough, when loaded with a bobbin, to hold the thread securely in place when you need both hands for some other task. For this reason I recommend beginners to obtain a bobbin holder.

Hackle Pliers: Spring steel hackle pliers are simple and inexpensive. Provided they have no sharp edges and the jaws meet properly to hold the hackle securely, there is not a lot that can go wrong with hackle pliers. When working with very soft hackles you can fit a small piece of rubber tubing – cycle valve rubber is ideal – over each of the jaws to avoid the hackle being cut by the metal serrations.

Another type of hackle pliers which is gaining popularity has a plastic body within which a retractable hook is held under spring tension. These work very well, and you may well prefer this type for handling smaller hackles. As hackle pliers are inexpensive, most fly tyers have both a large and a small pair.

Knife or Scalpel: A sharp penknife or a scalpel will be needed for cutting artificial materials against a straight edge, stripping the soft downy 'flue' from large feathers, and shearing the tying thread precisely where it emerges from the head of a fly. If you try to do this latter task with scissors you may risk cutting some of the hackles which have been tied close to the head to represent the legs of insects.

Scissors: If possible keep an old pair of scissors for cutting wire, tinsel, and the like, so that your best scissors are kept really sharp for the many fine cutting jobs which are part of fly-tying.

Dubbing Needle: The dubbing needle has several purposes. When you use fur to make the body of a fly, a process known as 'dubbing', the dubbing needle is used to prick out long fibres of fur from the body to represent the legs of an insect. Another important role for this tool is applying tiny drops of varnish to the heads of finished flies.

Getting Started

Ancient and Modern

The ancient tradition of fly tying grew up around the concept of creating the illusion of a real insect using naturally occurring materials such as fur, feathers and silk tied onto a fishing hook. Indeed, at one time all of the angler's tackle came from nature, with horsehair leaders, or casts as they were then termed, plaited silk lines, and wooden rods of greenheart or bamboo. Those days have gone, and we now mainly see carbon rods in use with plastic lines, nylon leaders and, not surprisingly, a wide range of man-made materials incorporated into modern artificial flies.

Many of the popular patterns of today make the best use of both natural and modern materials.

Tying Threads, Wire, Tinsels and Lurex: Nylon tying threads are available ready-waxed. They do not degrade unless left exposed to intense sunlight.

Keep any small electric motors or transformers, as they are a valuable source of fine copper wire. The insulating varnish on these wires can be useful in creating coloured body ribs; I have come across green, red, brown, orange and black finishes.

Polypropylene, Floss Silks and Chenille: You can use poly-propylene for tails, bodies and wings. At hay-making time you may be able to collect useful off-cuts in a variety of colours. Very fine polypropylene fibres are made as a substitute for seal's fur; they hold dyes of really bright shades, including fluorescents.

To avoid a tangled mass, keep coloured silks and chenilles in separately labelled envelopes.

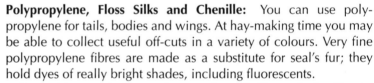

Feathers: Game birds' feathers are used a great deal in traditional trout and salmon flies. Domestic fowl also contribute, with both wing and neck feathers of chickens, geese, peafowl and ducks proving their worth. Natural moulting, road accidents and deaths inflicted by other predators mean that kingfisher, heron and owl feather, for example, are still obtainable, albeit in small quantities.

Furs: Natural furs remain important in fly tying. Of particular value are the skins of rabbit, mole, and seal. Old fur coats and stoles, worn out and beyond repair, are still of value to the fly tyer.

Basic Materials

Plastics: Braided mylar tubing, insulation stripped from off-cuts of telephone cables, and expanded polystyrene spheres are all useful materials. More importantly, their presence in your fly-tying kit can act as a trigger to your own creativity.

Polythene cut into narrow strips can be used to copy the translucence of the bodies of certain of the upwinged flies and their nymphs. Polythene is also used to represent the shell-like back of the freshwater shrimp.

Suggested Starter Kit

Purchased Materials

- Waxed tying thread in black, brown, yellow, red, orange, olive and purple
- Flat tinsel in silver and gold
- Oval tinsel in silver and gold
- Fine gold wire
- Fine lead wire
- Chenille in white, yellow, black
- Seal's fur, or artificial substitute, in olive, grey and black
- Natural hare's fur
- Rabbit's fur in blue-grey
- Calf tail in brown and orange
- Squirrel tail in natural and black
- Deer hair – natural and bleached white
- Cock hackles in black, natural red, dun, ginger, badger, furnace, Greenwell, blue dun, grizzle, bright blue and bright red
- Floss silk in black, cream and fluorescent white
- Peacock herl (or a complete tail feather)
- Mallard wing and breast feathers
- Pheasant tail feathers
- Golden pheasant tippet and topping feathers
- Teal feathers (barred)
- Goose wing feathers, natural white and dyed red
- Marabou plumes in black and red
- Polystyrene spheres
- Cellulose varnish/paints in clear, black, white and red
- Hooks in various sizes

Scavenged Materials

- Off-cuts of wool in as many colours as you can find
- Hen hackles in black and brown
- Turkey feathers in various shades
- Polythene sheeting
- Polythene tubing from used ballpoint pens
- Polypropylene twine
- Fine copper wire from old motors and transformers

Getting Started _____

Waterside Fly Tying

Angling literature is sprinkled with phrases like: '... had nothing in my fly box to match the hatch, so I went back to the car and tied up half a dozen...' Have you ever wondered how these fly fishers just happened to have the right tools and materials available in their car boot? And how did they tie flies without their fly-tying bench and chair? The answer, of course, is a portable fly-tying kit.

Designing a Portable Kit

Although some nice portable kits are available on the market, it is so much more satisfying to design your own. What you are doing is a packaging exercise: designing a carrying case so that tools and materials do not get damaged or mixed up when being moved from place to place.

The first step is to decide what tools and how much in the way of materials you intend taking with you. If you buy just the tools listed on page 14, then the answer will be simple: all of them. You will also want a small selection of hooks and tying materials. These you can top up periodically from your fly-tying 'base' camp. Lay out all these items to get an idea of how much space they take up.

Carrying Cases

A portable fly-tying outfit can be designed to fit in a plastic briefcase or a metal camera case, for example, but some of the nicest kits I have seen were housed in wooden boxes with hinged lids and secure catches. Rubber feet ensure the box does not scratch the surface of tables on which it is placed.

The Inserts

Decide how much of the area is needed for the tools, and cut a piece of plastic foam to the right size and thickness. (If you can get it, felt covering the foam enhances the appearance considerably.) Use a scalpel to make cut-outs in the shape of each tool so that they all fit snugly. A piece of foam in the lid will ensure that the tools do not jump out of position when the box is carried on its side.

The rest of the space is available to hold hooks and tying materials. Plastic containers can be stuck in place if you prefer but, apart from hooks, it may be better to have the flexibility of re-stocking your portable kit with different materials according to the venue you are going to visit.

A portable fly-tying kit.

If you are good at woodwork you may be able to include a few locking drawers in the front of your portable kit. In any case, I recommend you put your name, address and telephone number both outside and inside the box.

Where do you Fix the Vice?

It may be an obvious question, but if you are at the water's edge and you want to use your portable kit to tie an imitation of some insect you have seen on the water, how, exactly do you go about it? Well, the first thing is to go back to the car and get out your portable kit. Now if yours is a modern car it may not have a firm metal ledge above the number plate. In the past, there always was such a ledge and that was where tying vices of old were fixed. Instead, you could try the door flap of the glove box, many of which are designed to support cups of drinks. Of course, if you use a wooden box for your portable kit, you can fit it with a ledge on which to secure your vice.

Getting Started

What are we Trying to Imitate?

Even restricting our attention, in the first instance, to those artificial flies which are meant to represent real insects, the variety of sizes, shapes and colouring in nature is staggering. Then there are the many other food creatures – shrimps and small fishes, for example, on which trout will readily prey. Fortunately we need only concern ourselves with creatures large enough to be of interest to feeding trout, but that still leaves many thousands of creatures, and a great deal of scope for creative fly tying.

Not all the creatures on which trout feed are born and live around the waterside; some are 'terrestrials' which get blown off course and fall into the water. In autumn these terrestrials can account for a substantial proportion of the diet of trout on many rivers and lakes. Even so, averaged over the year it is the aquatic creatures which are of most importance, and so some understanding of the appearance and habits of their main groups, or orders, is obviously important to the fly tyer.

The Upwinged Flies

Upwinged insects lay their eggs on or in the water, usually in the afternoon and early evening. These eggs hatch into crawling or swimming nymphs depending upon the species. They live for about a year beneath the surface before hatching into duns – the first winged form of the adult fly. Within a day or so the dun sheds another coat and a bright 'spinner' emerges. It is the spinners which mate and lay eggs to continue the process. Fly tyers produce imitations of the nymph, the dun and the spinner of these flies.

Nymph and adult upwinged insect.

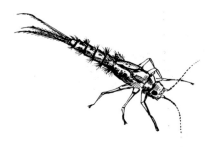

A Trout's Basic Diet

Sedge larva, pupa and adult.

The Sedge Flies

Sedge flies develop from eggs into larvae and then pupae. The flies have no dun stage, but their adult lives are in other respects as described for the upwinged flies. Most sedge flies are brown, many being mottled dark and light brown. They vary considerably in size, however, with the large sedges which emerge on warm summer evenings making a very welcome mouthful for trout on lakes and rivers. For best results, imitations of larvae, pupae and adult flies are needed.

The Chironomids

Buzzers, as they are sometimes known, are tiny flies which inhabit lakes and slow-flowing rivers. They can tolerate relatively high levels of pollution. Where they congregate on the windward side of a lake their tiny larvae and pupae are scooped up in huge numbers by surface-feeding trout.

Midge larva, pupa and adult.

The Stoneflies

These insects are an important food source for trout on many rough streams. They cannot tolerate pollution, and so their numbers act as a monitor of water quality. The large stonefly is a succulent and very distinctive nymph, and it is surprising that few close imitations have yet been produced. The nymphs crawl out of the water before hatching, and are extremely vulnerable to predation during this migration.

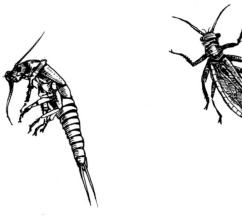

Stonefly nymph and adult.

The adult flies themselves are also copied, of course. In many species the male stoneflies cannot fly, and it is the egg-laying females which the fly tyer tries to copy. Most stoneflies continue beating their wings whilst laying their eggs, either touching them onto the surface or dropping them from just above the surface; and so artificial patterns generally take a fuzzy hackled form without the complication of wings.

Other Aquatic Creatures

Below the surface there is also much to interest the trout. Shrimps, snails, leeches, water boatmen and spiders all fall victim to feeding fish. Dragonflies and – more importantly on many stillwaters – damselflies are occasionally taken from the surface, yet it is the

20

Additions to a Trout's Diet

nymphs of these beautiful flies that feature more often on the trout's menu, and they seem particularly fond of damselfly nymphs. Small fishes are not given any special respect either; trout will even turn on fry of their own kind.

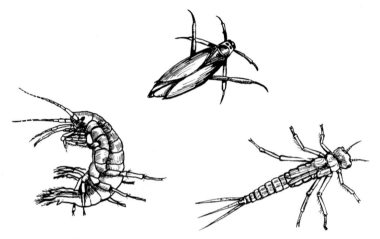

Shrimp, water boatman and damselfly nymph.

Terrestrials

Of the many land-based creatures which occasionally get blown on to the water, the hawthorn fly of spring and the large daddy-long-legs of late summer probably cause most excitement in the trout world. But beetles, ants and many other creatures do, on occasion, arrive on the water in numbers large enough for trout to seek them out in preference to their normal diet.

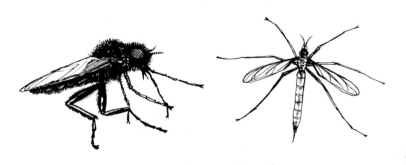

Hawthorn fly and daddy-long-legs.

BASIC TECHNIQUES

Building on a Firm Base

One of the important measures of fly quality is durability. Choice of materials plays a large part, of course, but an unsound foundation layer is often the Achilles' heel of cheap imported flies. If the foundation is not secure the whole fly can rotate around, or slide down, the shank of the hook.

Step 1: Wherever possible, set the hook in the vice so that the shank is horizontal and the point just obscured by the jaws of the vice. Exceptions are double and treble hooks, of course, but also certain types of barbless hooks, such as Roman Moser arrow-point hooks, whose points are flattened in the horizontal plane.

Step 2: Fit the spool between the spigots of the bobbin holder and feed the free end of the thread into the tube. If the thread refuses to slide right through the delivery tube you can help it on its way by sucking the far end of the tube.

Building the foundation layer.

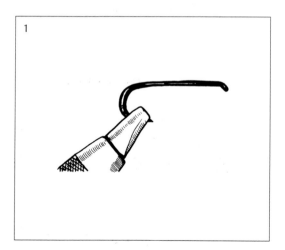

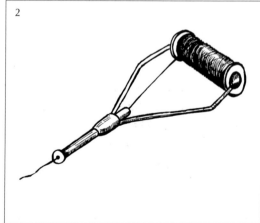

Foundation Layer

Step 3: Hold your wax in one hand with the required length of thread running beneath your thumb across the top of the wax. Pull the thread quickly across the wax which will melt and coat the thread. Reverse the direction of the thread and repeat the process to ensure that the thread is evenly coated.

Step 4: For most fly patterns you will need to start the foundation layer directly behind the eye of the hook, and to finish it where the bend begins – usually opposite the point of the hook. Although not strictly necessary on all fly patterns, it is good practice to wind foundation turns so that they are just touching one another. This makes a nice smooth surface on which to tie the other materials. Hold the free end of the thread below the hook and the bobbin holder above the hook. Bring the bobbin holder around behind the hook and trap the free end of the thread as you complete the turn. If you leave about 3in of tying thread as a free end, it can be used as a 'slide' for successive turns to slip down. This greatly speeds the process of building up a foundation layer.

Wind on all but the final three or four turns. Now trim off the loose end and add the last few turns. The wax will hold the tying thread reasonably well, but if you leave the bobbin holder hanging below the hook its weight will add security.

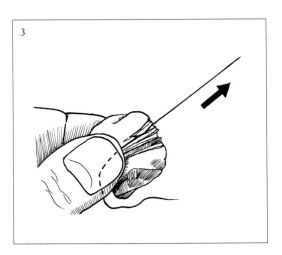

Tail Materials

wool tails

Tails are commonly made from feathers, wool or synthetic materials. Although these materials need different preparation they can all be tied on using one of a limited number of basic techniques. Before you first tie flies which use one of these types of tails, you might prefer to try out the method on a bare hook, complete with its foundation layer of course.

Feather Fibre Tails

trident tails

Strip off a few fibres from a pheasant tail feather by gripping the fibres firmly between forefinger and thumb and pulling them away from the feather stalk. Grasping the butts of the fibres, and with the fibre tips aligned, hold the tail along the top of the hook and adjust it to the required length. Then grip the hook shank and the feather fibres at the point where the foundation layer ends and draw the tying thread tight vertically above the hook. Trap the thread against the near side of the hook shank. Now pull the thread down loosely on the far side of the hook, again trapping it against the side of the hook so that a loop of thread is left above the tail. Pull the thread firmly until the loop disappears. This is called the 'pinch-and-loop' technique. Make two more such loops before releasing your grip, and the tail should be fixed securely.

forked tails

Forked Tails and Trident Tails

Stonefly nymphs have two tails and all upwinged nymphs have three tails. The strange thing is that in the majority of upwinged species the adult flies have only two tails.

One simple but very effective way of producing forked tails is to use the tip of a large cock hackle. Pull back the fibres as shown and cut off the hackle tip. Stroke back three or four fibres on either side of the hackle stalk and trim back the remainder. Now lay the hackle along the top of the hook and fix it in place using the pinch-and-loop technique. Finally, wind the tying thread between the two sets of fibres and around the hook shank enough times to set the tails at the angle you want.

feather fibre tails

Tails

Some species of upwinged flies and their nymphs have tails which fan out widely, while others, in common with the stoneflies, have narrow angles between their tails. It is doubtful whether a trout checks these angles before eating a fly, but it is a nice touch to get things more or less realistic if you can.

Trident tails are no more difficult. You simply pull out two sets of fibres on one side of the hackle and one set on the other. Leave the middle tail in line with the hook and set the others at equal angles on either side.

Pinch-and-loop technique.

After completing a fly with this type of tail, touch the tail roots and separating threads with a tiny spot of varnish to help keep them in position.

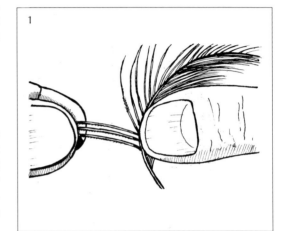

Wool Tails

For sea trout flies, synthetic material is often used in place of feathers because synthetic materials are so much more durable. (Sea trout have razor-sharp teeth and are notorious for nipping the tail of a fly.) Again, use the pinch-and-loop technique and trim the tail to size upon completion.

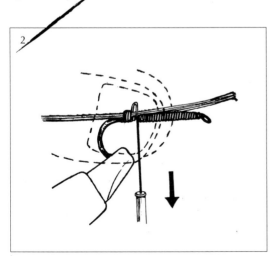

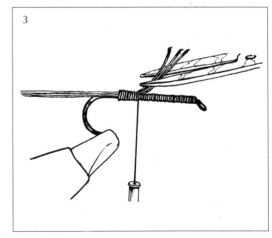

BASIC TECHNIQUES ─────────────

The Trout's 'Main Course'

To the trout, the body of the fly is the most important part. A fly with damaged tail, legs or wings is as acceptable as any other, but if the body does not pass muster then the trout will choose some other morsel and ignore your offering.

An insect's body is made up of two parts. The front, or thorax, is often thicker and darker than the rear, or abdomen, which usually tapers towards the tail. So, on some fly patterns we switch materials at the junction between abdomen and thorax.

Silk or Thread Bodies

Some of the best flies have plain tying thread bodies. They are easy to tie and, if you use nylon threads, reasonably durable.

Having tied in the tail (if required), wind back the tying thread in neat turns to a point about 1/8in from the eye of the hook, leaving room for tying in hackles, wings and head. Return the thread part way down to the bend, and again return to the front. Repeat this process to create the body shape you require.

Ribbed Bodies

A rib of tinsel or wire can be included in most types of bodies. The ribbing can be used to represent body segments, or it may simply be incorporated to improve durability.

Having tied in the tail, hold one end of the ribbing material beneath the hook and bring the tying thread round in two adjacent turns to trap it down. Now tie in the body material in the same manner – you may be using just the tying thread, of course. Wind the thread, and then the body material, forward along the hook shank to form the body. Use two or three turns of the tying thread to secure the body material and trim off the surplus. Next make neat, evenly-spaced turns of ribbing along the body of the fly, and again, secure the end under three turns of tying thread.

If only the abdomen is to be ribbed, the procedure is as above except that you stop the body dressing typically half-way between the bend and the eye of the hook. Then rib the abdomen and

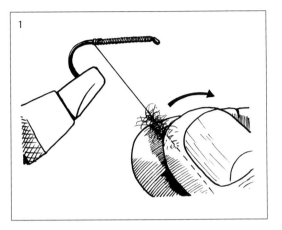

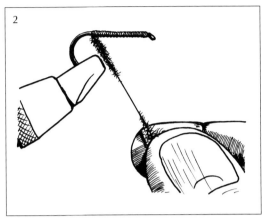

secure the ribbing before tying in the new body material, or continuing with the same material, according to the design of the fly.

Dubbing a fur body.

Many fly tyers wind on their ribbing in the opposite direction to
that used for the body. So, if you wind the body material clockwise
looking from the eye to the bend of the hook, then wind the ribbing
anti-clockwise.

Dubbed Bodies

Dubbing looks a complicated process, but in fact it is very easy. Fur,
wool or man-made fibres are made to adhere to a waxed thread,
which is then wound on to the shank of the hook to form a furry
body. Ribbing can, of course, be added afterwards.

With the foundation layer completed, take a small pinch of
dubbing material – rabbit's fur, for example – between thumb and
forefinger and slide it against the waxed tying thread. Roll the
thread between thumb and finger to spin the fibres onto the thread.
Slide this section of dubbing carefully up the thread until it just
touches the hook. Build up several sections of dubbing one below
the other until you have enough furry thread to be able to wind a
body. Give the fibres an extra roll at the junctions between the
sections. Before winding on the dubbing you can, if you wish, give
the foundation layer a wipe with varnish so that, once set, it will
grip the dubbing securely.

Dry-Fly Hackles

You will have tied a body, and the tying thread should be at the hackle position. Select a hackle whose fibre is about the same length as the gape of the hook. (To check fibre length bend the feather in a curve as shown.) Pull off the soft downy 'flue' from the base of the feather leaving only the upper, stiff fibres.

Lay the prepared hackle, shiny side up, along the top of the hook shank. Lock the hackle in place with three turns of thread and snip off the spare stalk just behind the eye. Now grasp the tip of the hackle with your hackle pliers and fold it forwards towards the eye of the hook so that on its release it remains at right angles to the hook shank.

The next stage is to wind on the hackle in close turns, making sure not to trap the fibres of the preceding turn. As you proceed, twist the hackle pliers if necessary to keep the shiny side of the fibres facing forwards. After two or three turns, bring the tying thread over the hackle tip and lock it in place with two turns of the thread.

The final stage is to pull back the hackle fibres towards the bend of the hook and make two or three turns with the tying thread just behind the hackles. This will give the hackles a slight backward rake.

What is a Hackle?

A hackle is a neck feather, usually from a cockerel or a game bird. Hackle feathers can be tied to represent the legs or the breathing filaments of an insect. They can also be used as wings, particularly on large flies such as the Daddy-long-legs, or as 'beards' on certain types of wet flies.

Cock hackles, being shiny and stiff, are invariably used when tying dry flies; they help ensure the fly sits up well on the surface. The softer hen hackles are sometimes used when tying wet flies, although many fly tyers use cock hackles for both wet and dry patterns.

On wet flies the hackle is usually tied in before the wings are put on; but there are a few exceptions. On most dry flies the hackle is put on after the wing, although at least part of the hackle is generally tied in behind the wing.

Dry-fly hackle.

Hackles

Wet-Fly Hackles

Again get to the stage where the body is complete. Select a soft hackle whose fibres are just a little longer than the distance from the eye to the point of the hook. Having removed the flue, grip the root of the hackle with your pliers and, holding the tip of the hackle, stroke the hackle fibres back towards the root of the hackle. Now tie in the tip, locking it in place with three turns of tying thread, before winding the thread up to the eye. Hold the hackle away from the hook shank with the shiny side forward. Fold the soft hackle double on itself, so that all fibres face towards the rear of the fly. Now carefully wind turns of doubled hackle around the hook shank in close, but not overlapping, turns. Lock in the hackle with three turns of tying thread before trimming off the unwanted stalk.

Wet-fly hackle (below left).
Beard hackle (below).

Beard Hackles

Prepare the fly up to completion of the body, but do not tie in the wing yet. Pull off a bunch of long fibres from a cock hackle of the required colour and adjust them until the tips align. Hold this bunch underneath the hook in front of the body so that the hackle tips just reach the hook point. Tie in with three turns of tying thread.

Basic Techniques

Why Bother With Wings?

If pressed, plenty of fly tyers would have to admit that they find the process of winging difficult – so much so that many avoid it altogether. Once you have mastered the pinch-and-loop technique – described earlier – wings should pose little difficulty.

The only significant difference between most dry and wet-fly feather wings is in the preparation of the material; and hair wings are, in many respects, even easier to tie.

Matched Wet-Fly Wings

Many traditional wet-fly patterns call for this style of winging, for which wing quill feathers are normally used. It is important to select a matching pair of feathers – one from each wing of the bird – and to tie them in with the shiny side out.

Tie the fly up to the point where the body and hackle are complete. Next use your dubbing needle to select a pair of matching sections from each feather. Cut the sections away from the quill, being careful to keep the fibres 'married' together. Align the wing tips and position them so that they extend just to the bend of the hook. (There will be occasions when you may want to vary this, for example in low-water salmon and sea trout flies where the

Matched wet-fly wings.

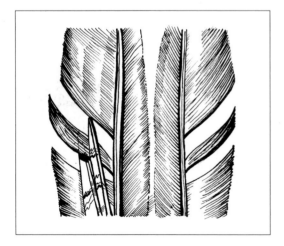
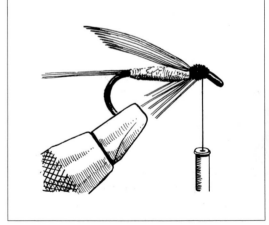

Wet-Fly Wings

body and wings are tied much shorter than usual.) Tie in the wings using the pinch-and-loop method.

Hair Wings

Traditional fully-dressed salmon flies take a long time to tie, but their hair-winged equivalents have been found to be just as effective in luring both salmon and sea trout. Here we will tie a wing consisting of just two components, a red underwing and a black overwing, so that the wing extends about half a hook length beyond the bend.

matched wet-fly wings

Having first tied the body, and with the throat hackle already in place, select a small bunch of red calf tail hair. Align the tips before tying in the bunch with four or five tight turns of tying thread. Finally, select, align and tie in a smaller bunch of black calf tail hair, again binding it down securely with four or five turns of tying thread.

Streamer Wings

Streamer flies are lures or fish imitators, and they offer great scope for creativity in fly tying. Streamer wings vary from just a matching pair of hackle feathers to a complex sandwich of furs and feathers of various colours. They are all quite easy to tie.

hair wings

Once you have tied the body and added the hackle, you are ready to tie on the various parts which make up the streamer wing. Let us assume your wing will consist of a pair of large red hackles faced on either side by smaller blue ones. The longer, inner hackles should be sized to extend beyond the hook bend by up to one hook length. (Longer wings are not only less durable but they also result in missed takes as the trout seize the end of the wing without engulfing the hook.)

Select and strip off the flue from the hackles, and place the inner wing hackles in position on top of the hook, shiny sides out. Tie them in using the pinch-and-loop method, and cut off the excess hackle stalk. Place a blue hackle on each side of the wing, again with the shiny side out, and make three tight turns with the tying thread before cutting off the surplus stalks.

streamer wings

31

Can a Trout see the Wings of a Floating Fly?

Wings certainly make dry flies look more realistic to us, but do the trout actually see the wings? Well, the wings of a spent spinner lie flat on the surface and are clearly visible from below; but the wings of a dun, drifting along in the current, will also be visible to trout lying deep in the water and to one side of the path of the drift. So, winging is probably worthwhile for all spinners *and* for duns which are to be fished in deep water.

Spent spinner wings.

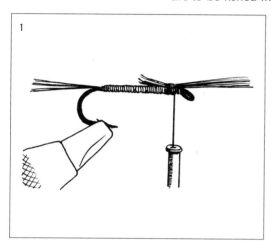

Spent Spinner Wings

Tie on the wings before building up the body. Take two small hackles and strip off the flue and lower fibres to a point which leaves wings of the required length – about one to one-and-a-half hook gapes is usually about right. Place the hackles upon the hook, one on top of the other with the shiny side up, with the hackle tips facing forward. Secure with three turns of tying thread and cut off the surplus hackle stalk.

Now bring the tying thread in front of the wings. Part the wings, pulling the wing nearest

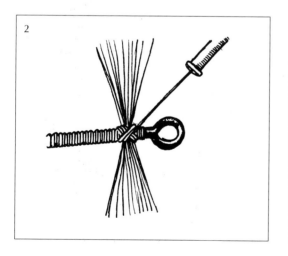

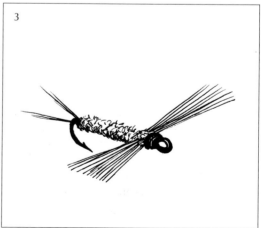

Dry-Fly Wings

to you out at right angles to the hook shank. Take the tying thread up in front of the wing, over the hook shank and *behind* the far wing. Bring the silk under the hook *behind* the near wing. Now pull out the far wing at right angles to the hook shank and take the silk *in front* of the far wing and down, under the hook shank again. Repeat this figure-of-eight tying twice more and the wings will remain at right angles to the hook.

Incidentally, when tying spent spinners, a short softish hackle is preferable so that the fly will sink into the surface film rather than riding high like a living fly.

Fan-winged Mayfly.

Mayfly Fan Wings

Having tied a body, leaving enough room for wings, hackle and head, select a matching pair of mallard breast feathers. Trim off the flue and surplus fibre until the wing is about the same length as the hook. Place the wings, convex surfaces together, along the top of the hook shank and tie them in using the pinch-and-loop method. Pull down each wing stalk on its corresponding side of the hook shank until the wings tilt upwards. Now, gripping the wings to hold them in position, bring the tying thread in front of the wings and make four tight turns before cutting off the surplus stalks. The hackle can now be added to complete the fly.

Split Wings

Split wings can be tied in the 'upright' or the 'advanced' position. The tying process is much the same in each case.

Cut two long matching sections from a pair of wing quill feathers. Place them together on top of the hook shank with the tips aligned. Adjust for the required wing length before locking them in position with three pinch-and-loop turns. If upright wings are required, carefully pull back the wings to the required angle and wind four tight turns of tying thread close in front of the wings. You can spread the wings further by making figure-of-eight turns with the tying thread, passing it between the wings each time. Finally, trim off the surplus material at the wing base, tapering it so that you can trap it with the tying thread. Complete the body and hackle.

Split-winged dry flies.

33

Basic Techniques ————————————————

Forming the Head

Some fly tyers use half-hitches to secure each tying stage, rather than relying on well-waxed thread and the weight of the bobbin holder. On large flies the penalty in terms of neatness may be minimal, but when tying smaller flies the bulk of all the knots soon begins to show. Nowhere is this more noticeable than at the head of the fly, where body and ribbing materials, wings and hackles are all finally tied off. The result is often a large and unsightly head, which may also reduce the hooking power of the fly.

If you have been securing your materials as suggested in the preceding topics, the final step to a well-dressed fly is to build a neat, well-shaped head using close turns of the tying thread. You are then ready to make your one and only knot.

The Whip Finish

Step 1:   Using the forefinger and centre finger of your right hand (left-handed tyers should read left for right, and vice versa) make a triangle with the tying thread, returning it to the bobbin holder just below the tail of the fly. Turn your right wrist away from you, using the forefinger to carry the thread over the head of the fly, trapping the free (bobbin) end of the thread. Use your right centre finger to push the thread over and down on the far side of the head. Carry both fingers down below the fly and return to the starting position.

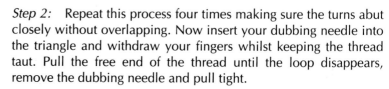

Step 2:   Repeat this process four times making sure the turns abut closely without overlapping. Now insert your dubbing needle into the triangle and withdraw your fingers whilst keeping the thread taut. Pull the free end of the thread until the loop disappears, remove the dubbing needle and pull tight.

Step 3:   Use your scalpel to cut off the thread hard against the knot. Give the completed head a coat of varnish, allow it to dry and then apply a second coat. This gives the head of the fly a neat and secure finish.

Please don't be put off – the whip finish is not as difficult as it sounds. If you prefer, you can buy a whip-finish tool which is used

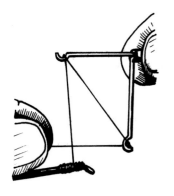

Whip-finish tool.

Heads, and the Whip Finish

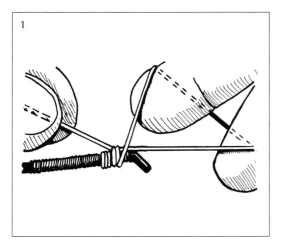

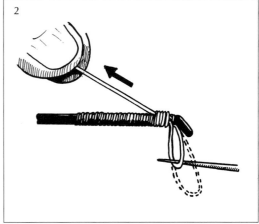

The whip finish.

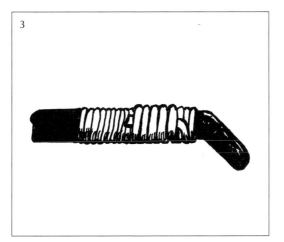

in place of the fingers of the right hand and the dubbing needle. Some people find it easier to see what they are doing when using a whip-finish tool, but most experienced fly tyers find they can work much faster with just their hands.

SIMPLE NYMPHS AND HACKLED FLIES ⎯⎯

Origin

Anglers use the term Black Gnat to describe a number of terrestrial flat winged flies (diptera). On many rivers and streams the most common of these insects is a small fly called *Bibio johannis*. These flies fall or get blown on to the water and trout are very partial to them. The Black Gnat is also a pattern worth trying near the reedy margins of lakes. The tying below is one of the simplest of all dry flies, but very effective as a tempter of trout.

Materials

Hook   Size 16 fine wire
Tying thread   Black
Body   Black tying thread
Hackle   Black cock
Head   Black tying thread

Tying Hints

Step 1:   Wind a foundation layer beginning at the eye and continuing to the bend. Wind back the thread in close turns to the hackle position to produce a body with just two layers of thread. (The fly you are imitating has a long thin body.)

Step 2:   Select a good cock hackle with short stiff fibres. Remove the flue and unwanted lower fibres and tie in the hackle stalk on top of the hook, using the pinch-and-loop method. Secure with two more tight turns of tying thread.

Step 3:   To aid buoyancy, give this fly four complete turns of hackle working forwards towards the eye of the hook. Lock in the hackle and trim off the excess.

Step 4:   Finish by tying and whip-finishing a small neat head. After the head varnish has dried, dip the fly into dry-fly floatant so that the oil impregnates the tying thread. This will ensure that your Black Gnat floats well even in turbulent water.

Fishing Tips

There are hatches of various species of small black diptera both in spring and again in autumn when, on breezy days, your Black Gnat should prove most useful. Don't worry unduly if your fly gets drowned in extremely turbulent water, as this is sometimes the fate of the natural insect which gets trapped in the surface film.

Hackled Black Gnat

Variations on a Theme

To improve the buoyancy of this fly you can include a short tail of stiff cock hackle fibres.

Mating Black Gnats can be imitated with the Knotted Midge, which is tied as above except that an additional hackle, smaller than the head hackle, is tied in at the bend of the hook.

Tying the Black Gnat.

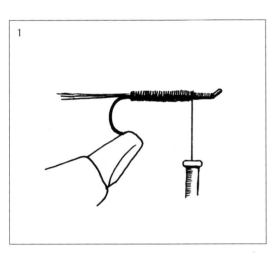

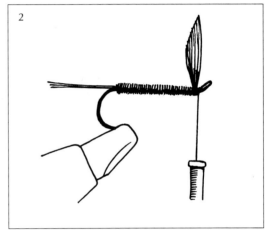

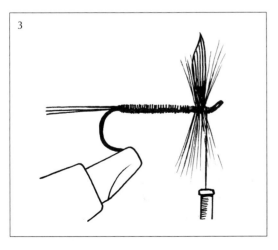

Simple Nymphs and Hackled Flies ___

Origin

The Grey Duster is a very old and versatile fly pattern. It is classed as a 'general representation' of several kinds of flies rather than a close imitation of one particular species. Tied on hooks as small as size 16 it can be used to imitate the *Caenis,* or Anglers' Curse – a tiny upwinged fly – and it may also take trout which are feeding on midges. In sizes 12 and 14 it is often acceptable as an imitation of various olive duns and of most species of stoneflies. Indeed, when autumn hatches of stoneflies are at their peak I know of no more effective dry-fly pattern.

The mayfly spinner, sometimes known as the 'greydrake', can also be copied with a Grey Duster in size 10. The body is a little dark, perhaps, but once the trout are well 'on to' the mayfly they seem quite free of colour prejudice: the Grey Duster is the right size and shape, and will do nicely!

Tying the Grey Duster.

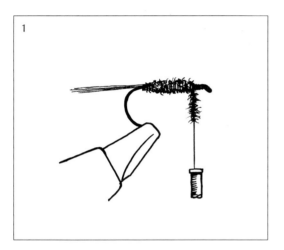

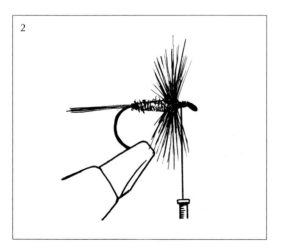

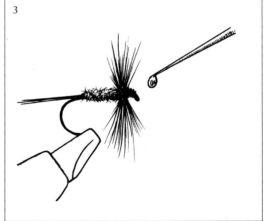

Grey Duster

Materials

Hook   Size 10 to 16 fine wire
Tying thread   Brown
Body   Dubbed blue-grey rabbit's fur
Hackle   Badger cock

Tying Hints

Step 1:   Wind a foundation layer of tying thread from eye to hook bend, and make sure the thread is well waxed before dubbing on the rabbit fur. Tie a neat, carrot-shaped body taper leaving enough room for three turns of hackle and a neat head.

Step 2:   Select a hackle with strong markings. The hackle fibres should be a little longer than the gape of the hook. Wind three turns of hackle, four if you intend fishing very turbulent water.

Step 3:   Wind tying thread to form the head and use the whip finish to secure it. Give the head two coats of clear varnish, allowing time for the varnish to dry between coats.

Variations on a Theme

The Grey Duster is sometimes tied with a tail. This consists of four or five well-marked fibres from a badger cock hackle. The tail should be just a little longer than the hook shank.

Fishing Tips

When imitating stoneflies, a well-oiled fly is essential to copy the habit the female flies have of just touching down on to the water to lay their eggs.

Drowning Mayfly spinners can be imitated by allowing the Grey Duster to sink into the surface film. On turbulent water this is an excellent means of reducing the problem of 'drag', because the partly-drowned fly acts rather like a sea anchor.

SIMPLE NYMPHS AND HACKLED FLIES ___

Origin

This fly has been doing service on both chalk streams and rough streams for well over 100 years. It vies with the Pheasant Tail Nymph as the most popular general nymph representation – popular with trout as well as anglers. The GRHE is an excellent imitation of emerging upwinged flies such as the Medium Olive.

Materials

Hook   Sizes 12 to 16 forged
Tail   Hare's body fur
Body   Hare's body fur dubbed onto tying thread
Rib   Flat gold tinsel over abdomen
Thorax   Dubbed hare's body fur, pricked out at the sides to represent legs
Head   Brown tying thread

Tying Hints

The fur used in most dressings of this nymph is, in fact, body fur, rather than the shorter fibred hare's ear fur.

Step 1:   Prepare the hook in the usual way, running waxed thread from eye to hook bend. For the tail, select a few of the longer fibres called 'guard hairs'. Catch in with tying thread, and then tie in a short length of flat gold tinsel. Tinsel is preferable to lurex, as the metal rib is stronger and adds a little weight to this sinking pattern.

Step 2:   The next task is to dub on a body of brown hare's fur. Wind the dubbed thread as far as the thorax and lock it in position. Rib the abdomen with four turns of ribbing wound in the opposite direction to the dubbing. Tie off the tinsel ribbing and remove the excess. Dub more fur onto the tying thread and wind a slightly humped thorax. Make a neat head, whip-finish and varnish.

Step 3:   To complete, use a dubbing needle to prick out fibres from the thorax and sides of the body to create a nymph-like form.

Gold Ribbed Hare's Ear (GRHE)

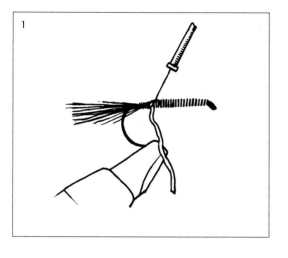

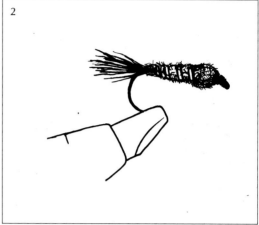

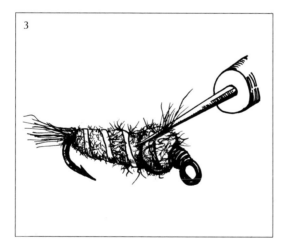

Tying a Gold Ribbed Hare's Ear.

Variations on a Theme

The GRHE can be weighted to help it sink more quickly in fast flowing water. Wings are sometimes added to make a dry fly which, in my experience, is best fished 'damp' – that is, partly submerged in the surface film.

41

Simple Nymphs and Hackled Flies

Origin

Buzzers, or chironomids, are those tiny flies which appear in vast swarms on most stillwaters towards evening. They do not bite, unlike the tiny highland gnats which have miniature chain-saws concealed in their jaws. Dr H A Bell developed the original Blagdon Buzzer; it is an imitation of a midge pupa, and probably the most important nymph of all as far as stillwater anglers are concerned.

Tying a Midge pupa.

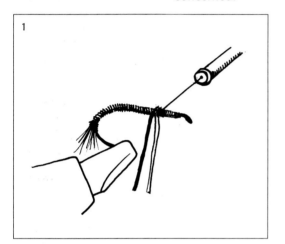

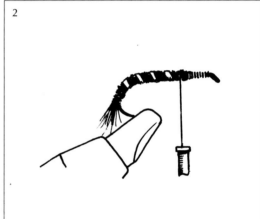

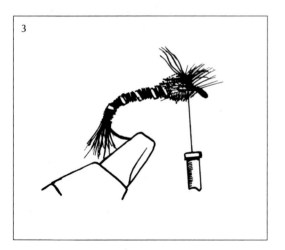

Buzzer

Materials

Hooks   Sizes 10 to 14 forged
Tail   White fluorescent floss silk
Body   Black floss silk
Ribbing   Flat gold tinsel
Thorax   Bronze peacock herl
Breathing filaments   White fluorescent floss silk
Head   Black tying thread

Tying Hints

Step 1:   Unlike most other fly patterns, the foundation layer should be taken part way round the bend to imitate the natural curved form of the midge pupa. Tie in the tail and then run the thread back to the thorax position to tie in both the body floss and the ribbing tinsel. Bring the thread right back to the tail position trapping the body and ribbing materials.

Step 2:   Now for the body itself. Return the thread to the thorax position, wind on the body floss and lock it off. Next wind the ribbing tinsel around the body in a spiral until it reaches the thorax position. If you wound the body floss clockwise then wind the ribbing anti-clockwise, as this will make it stand out better. Tie off the tinsel.

Step 3:   Now we add the thorax and breathing filaments. Tie in a short length of white floss together with three strands of peacock herl. Wind the peacock herl on top of the white floss to form a humped thorax. Lock off both floss and peacock herl so that the floss, which will represent the breathing filaments, extends over the eye of the hook.

Step 4:   The final job is to tie the head. Draw back the silk floss as you wind tying thread to form a small neat head. Whip-finish the head and give it two coats of varnish. Trim the tail and the breathing filament floss to a length of $1/8$in and the Buzzer is complete.

Fishing Tips

Midge pupae are at their most vulnerable when they make the journey to the surface. The pupae drift gently up to the surface where the survivors struggle to break through the surface film. Many do not make it, especially if the water is very choppy or if a flat calm has allowed an oily film to form. At this stage trout patrol just below the surface, sipping in huge quantities of hatching midges.

The Buzzer can be fished just below the surface by greasing all but the last 3in of leader. If there is a slight ripple, an occasional twitch of the fly line is enough to attract attention. In flat calm conditions it is usually better to fish the Buzzer static in the surface film. An alternative tactic is to degrease the leader and allow the Buzzer to sink very slowly. Using this technique you should be ready for takes 'on the drop', as a trout seizes the Buzzer some distance below the surface.

SIMPLE NYMPHS AND HACKLED FLIES ___

Origin

The original Zulu design is at least three hundred years old. As an imitative pattern this wet fly is reputed to be a beetle representation. The Zulu has the distinction of having been banned at one time from use in competitions on account of its effectiveness.

The Zulu is also a useful sea trout fly, particularly when fished on the top dropper in a team of two or three flies. It is tied with a 'palmered' body. The term palmer was used to describe pilgrims returning with palm leaves from the Holy Land.

Materials

Hook   Sizes 8 to 14 forged
Tying thread   Black
Body   Black seal's fur
Rib   Flat silver tinsel
Hackle   Black cock
Head   Black tying thread

Tying Hints

Step 1:   Prepare the foundation layer as usual. Then, at the bend of the hook, tie in a length of tinsel and the red wool tail. Dub on the seal's fur and wind a neat body.

Step 2:   Select a hackle with fibres one-and-a-half times the gape of the hook. Tie in the hackle at the head position and wind six or eight turns of hackle around the hook shank taking each turn *behind* the last. The first two turns should be close together, but space the others out along the body of the fly. Lock the hackle in place at the tail using the ribbing tinsel, and then run the ribbing up the body. If you wound the hackle clockwise, then run the ribbing anti-clockwise, making sure you free any fibres which are in danger of being trapped under the tinsel.

Step 3:   Trim the tail to length. A neat whip-finished head and two coats of varnish will complete the fly.

Variations on a Theme

Almost as widely used as the Black Zulu is the Blue Zulu, a variant with a blue palmered hackle. The above palmering technique is used in several traditional patterns, the oldest of which is the Soldier Palmer which is tied with a scarlet wool tail and scarlet seal's fur body with gold ribbing and a red cock hackle.

Tying the Zulu.

Fishing Tips

On reservoirs the Zulu is a useful top dropper fly. Fished dibbling the surface on breezy days it attracts attention and is often taken right alongside the boat.

As a river trout fly I find the Zulu is most effective when tied in size 14, but for sea trout a more substantial version is usually required. Size 8 is not too big for fishing in the dead of night when your fly may well be taken just as you are about to lift it from the water.

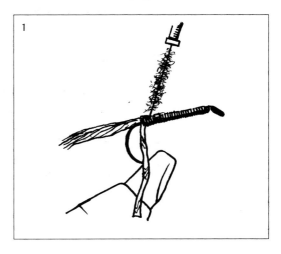

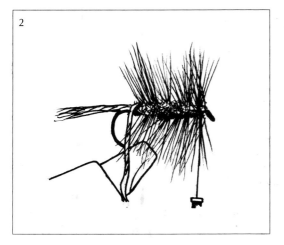

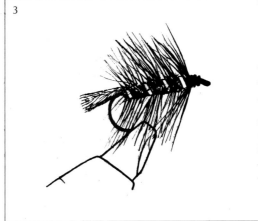

SIMPLE NYMPHS AND HACKLED FLIES ——

Origin

This famous old Welsh pattern is the emblem of The Welsh Salmon and Trout Angling Association. Spelt correctly – and traditionally it is not! – the name Coch-a-bon-ddu means 'red with black trunk'.

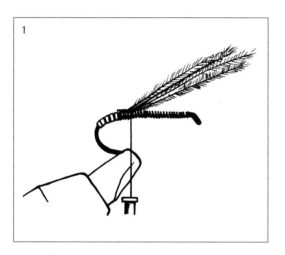

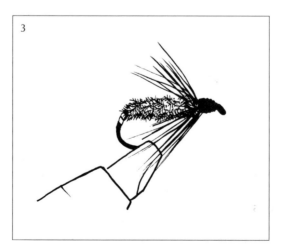

Tying the Coch-y-bonddhu.

Coch-y-bonddhu

This is a description which fits several species of beetles, and particularly the garden chafer which first appears in late spring or early summer. Certainly as a general purpose beetle imitator this is a most killing summer pattern.

Materials

Hooks   Sizes 12 to 16 forged
Tying thread   Black
Tag   Fine gold tinsel
Body   Peacock herl
Hackle   'Coch-y-bonddhu' or furnace cock hackle (a red hackle with black centre and fibre tips)
Head   Black tying thread

Tying Hints

Step 1:   Wind on the foundation layer from eye to bend. Tie in a slip of gold tinsel and four fibres of peacock herl. Wrap the tinsel around the hook to form a gold tag. Tie down the tinsel and trim off the surplus before running the tying thread back down the hook.

Step 2:   Next form the body of the fly by wrapping turns of peacock herl in tight spirals around the hook up to the head position. Lock in the peacock herl and trim off the excess.

Step 3:   Finally, wind on three turns of hackle and finish the fly with a head of tying thread. Whip-finish and varnish the head.

Variations on a Theme

Peacock herl is not very strong, and the Coch-y-bonddhu is soon destroyed by the teeth of trout. A wipe of varnish along the foundation layer greatly improves the durability of this fly.

For the wet-fly version of the Coch-y-bonddhu soft hen hackles are preferable to stiff cock hackles. To provide for more rapid sinking, use no more than two turns of hackle in the wet version.

Fishing Tips

This is a great fly for fly-fishing on mountain streams, where it is readily accepted by wild brown trout feeding on terrestrial creatures blown in on the wind. Indeed, on both upland and lowland rough streams, when brown trout are feeding just below the surface in fast water, the Coch-y-bonddhu is usually an acceptable offering.

As a lake fly the Coch-y-bonddhu is well worth a try on the top dropper, particularly as evening approaches.

SIMPLE NYMPHS AND HACKLED FLIES ___

Origin

Primarily a stillwater pattern, this extremely effective lure was devised in 1971 by Brian Kench for fishing on Ravensthorpe reservoir. It may well be taken by trout feeding on the fry of roach and other coarse fish with highly reflective flanks. It is also thought to be a reasonable imitation of certain large sedge pupae, particularly when tied with peach or orange wool.

Tying the Baby Doll.

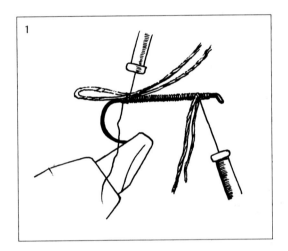

Materials

Hook   Long shank sizes 6 to 10
Tying thread   Black
Body   White nylon Sirdar baby wool
Tail   White, orange, green or yellow wool
Head   Black tying thread

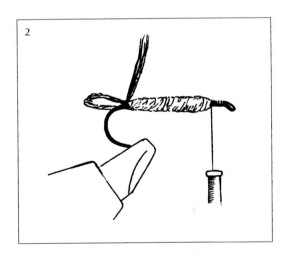

Baby Doll

Tying Hints

Step 1:   Start by locking the tying thread at the bend of the hook, leaving a free end a few inches long. Fold each of two lengths of wool double and tie them in at the tail, with the longer ends towards the eye of the hook. This wool will form the tail and back of the fly. Run the tying thread to the head and tie in a further length of wool, leaving enough room for the head of the fly.

Step 2:   Wind the body wool in neat turns around the prepared hook shank to build up a body. Use the free end of tying thread to lock in the body wool, and then bring the two longer loose ends of tail wool over the top of the body and trap them in behind the eye.

Step 3:   Wind and whip-finish the head and apply two coats of varnish. Cut the tail to length.

Variations on a Theme

Versions of this pattern use fluorescent day-glo nylon wool, and the body and back/tail colours can be switched to green, orange or whatever. As a fry imitator there is some virtue in using a green or brown wool to represent the back of the fish. You could even add a few red or orange hackles as pectoral fins. I think there is some merit in adding a splash of red either at throat or tail to indicate a wounded fish; trout show no mercy towards the infirm.

The all-black version of the Baby Doll goes by the name of the Undertaker.

Fishing Tips

As a fry imitator, this fly should be fished with an erratic but continuous retrieve. It is worth a try when trout are feeding on small fry in the margins, but I find it performs best at greater depths where less light penetrates.

To represent an emerging sedge pupa the Baby Doll should be fished right on the bottom and given a twitching retrieve – an inch or two at a time – once every three or four seconds.

WINGED FLIES

Origin

At the mention of the word mayfly even those professing not to know a moth from a midge are certain to think of fly fishing. And so, it appears, it has always been; for imitations of the mayfly are mentioned in the earliest literature of our sport. The term 'greendrake' was applied to the dun stage, while the spinner was often referred to as the 'greydrake'.

Materials

Hook   Size 10 fine wire
Tying thread   Brown
Tail   Three cock pheasant tail fibres
Body   Cream floss silk
Ribbing   Brown tying thread
Wings   Mallard breast feathers
Hackle   Dun cock hackle
Head   Brown tying thread

Tying Hints

Step 1:   Prepare the foundation layer leaving 6in of spare thread at the tail. Tie in the tail fibres and run the tying thread to the head. Wind on a neat, tapering body of floss silk and lock off at the head.

Step 2:   Rib the body with the spare end of tying thread, making two sets of three turns close together just above the tail; continue ribbing with equally spaced turns to represent the body segments. The wider ribs at the tail end of the body correspond to dark brown markings on the last two body segments of the natural mayfly.

Step 3:   The next step is to add the wings. Take a matching pair of mallard breast feathers and remove the flue and spare fibres to leave wings of one and a third times the body length. Place the feathers back to back and use the pinch-and-loop method to lock them into place. Secure with two further turns of tying thread. Carefully pull the feathers to the vertical and wind three turns of

---

Fishing Tips

This fly achieves deception not only because it looks something like the real thing, but also because it behaves so naturally, alighting gently onto the water like an egg-laying spinner or a dun needing a second attempt to take-off. For this reason it is very important to cast gently, and for most of us that means not trying to cover fish at too great a range. Once the trout are really 'on' the mayfly, and provided the natural hatch is not so profuse that the trout are too spoilt for choice, this hackled imitation is a deadly pattern. If Red Indian stalking tactics can get you within ten or twelve yards of your quarry unseen, and provided you can place your fly reasonably accurately in front or just to one side of him, a response is almost assured.

Fan-Winged Mayfly

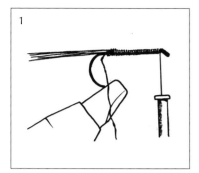

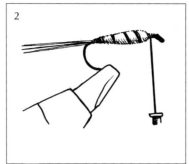

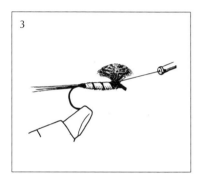

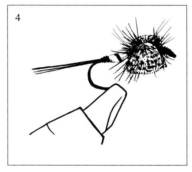

Tying a Fan-Winged Mayfly.

tying thread close behind the wings. Now part the wings and run the tying thread in figure-of-eight turns around the wing bases to secure them in the fanned position.

Step 4: The hackle is added next. Wind two turns behind the wings and another turn in front. Secure the hackle and trim off the excess hackle and wing stalks. Wind a neat head, whip-finish, and apply two coats of head varnish.

This is a fly which will benefit greatly from an application of dry-fly floatant well before you cast it on to the water.

Variations on a Theme

Teal or wood duck feathers can be used to make the wings. For greater realism they can be dyed green or yellow to represent duns and grey or black for spinners.

WINGED FLIES

Fishing Tips

This is a nymph for all seasons; however, as upwinged flies are particularly abundant in spring, I would definitely not be without the PTN on opening day. Fished up and across stream in fast water it will be given life by the conflicting surface currents. Just watch for a splash or a pull on the leader and tighten at once.

Frank Sawyer and Oliver Kite publicized the induced take method which they perfected on the chalk streams of southern England. Cast a weighted PTN upstream and to one side of a nymphing trout. The nymph sinks towards the river bed as it drifts down to where the trout is feeding. As the nymph comes alongside the trout, raise your rod to give a slight pull on the line; then the PTN will rise towards the surface like a hatching nymph – an action which trout find hard to resist.

Origin

If anyone was to ask what colour are the majority of nymphs of the upwinged flies, I would have to describe them as dark brown, often with lighter brown patches… in fact very much like a pheasant's tail feathers. The original idea for this classic pattern is attributed to Payne Collier, around the turn of the century. Nowadays the Pheasant Tail Nymph is dressed in many ways, from Frank Sawyer's simple but highly successful copper wire and pheasant tail fibre creations to the more elegant dressings used by some modern stillwater anglers. The pattern below is tied by Derek Hoskin.

Materials

Hooks   Sizes 10 to 16 forged
Tying thread   Black
Tail   Three pheasant tail feather fibres
Abdomen   Pheasant tail fibres
Thorax   Blue-grey rabbit's fur, dubbed on with tying thread
Wingcase   Pheasant tail fibres doubled over the thorax
Head   Black tying thread

Tying Hints

Step 1:   Make the foundation layer and tie in three pheasant tail fibres as tails. Next, tie in a bunch of about six pheasant tail fibres, run the thread back to the thorax position and wind a carrot-shaped abdomen. Lock down the fibres and pull the free ends back towards the tail of the nymph.

Step 2:   Dub guard hairs (the longer hairs) from the rabbit's fur on to the thread before building up a slightly humped thorax. Carry the pheasant tail fibres forward over the top of the thorax and tie them in at the front of the fly.

Step 3:   Wind a neat head and tie off with a whip finish. Prick out a few of the guard hairs from the thorax to represent legs. Apply two coats of varnish to the head and the PTN is complete.

Pheasant Tail Nymph (PTN)

Variations on a Theme

The most important variant of this pattern is the weighted version.
(Various methods of weighting flies are discussed in a later topic.) A
heavily weighted PTN is ideal for fishing the 'induced take' tactic.

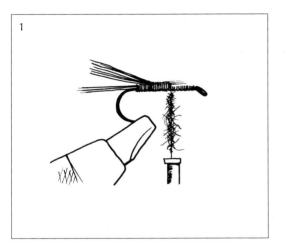

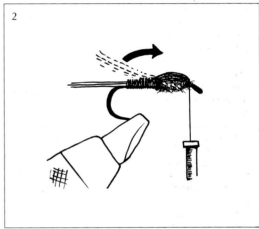

Tying a Pheasant Tail Nymph.

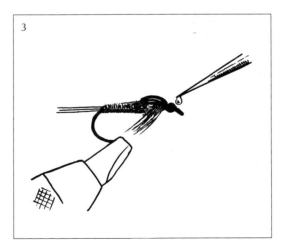

WINGED FLIES

Origin

This fly was originally called Moon's Fly, after a Mr Moon, a butcher from Tunbridge Wells. Mr Moon, with his friend Mr Dewhurst, devised the pattern in the early eighteenth century. Sometime later it was renamed after the trade of its inventor.

Materials

Hook   Sizes 10 to 16 forged, for trout
          Sizes 6 to 12 forged, for sea trout
Tying thread   Black
Tail   Red Ibis or dyed goose
Body   Flat silver tinsel
Rib   Oval silver tinsel
Wing   Blue-black mallard wing
Throat hackle   Black cock
Head   Black tying thread

Tying Hints

Step 1:   After making the foundation layer, take a thin slip of tail feather, being careful to keep the fibres 'married' together. Use the pinch-and-loop method to tie in the tail slip.

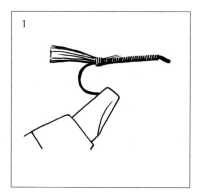
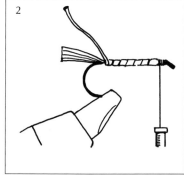

Tying the Butcher.

54

_ Matched Wet Wings – The Butcher

Step 2: Tie in a length of oval tinsel and then run the tying thread back to the head position; there tie in a length of flat tinsel and wind it in neat overlapping turns down to the tail and back. Lock off the flat tinsel and wind the oval tinsel rib up to the head position. Lock in the rib and trim off any excess.

Step 3: Now tie in a bunch of black cock hackle fibres in the throat position beneath the hook.

Step 4: The next step is to add the wings. These are made from two slips of blue mallard wing feathers, one from each wing of the bird. Place the wing slips together and carefully align the tips before using the pinch-and-loop method to lock the wings in place.

Step 5: A neat head and whip finish, with two coats of head varnish, and the Butcher is ready for work.

Variations on a Theme

For sea trout fishing, the wing slips should be very sparse and a dozen fibres will suffice for the throat hackle; otherwise you may obscure most of the light reflecting properties of the ribbed silver body.

The Gold Butcher is dressed as above but with gold tinsel in place of silver. The Bloody Butcher has a scarlet throat hackle in place of the black, while the Kingfisher Butcher has a blue tail, a gold body and an orange throat hackle.

Fishing Tips

Fished on the point of a team of wet flies the Butcher scores well when rivers and streams are clearing after a spate. It seems likely that trout take it in mistake for a small fish. It is also popular as a trout fly in Scotland where it deceives many a fine loch trout.

During the low water conditions of mid-summer the Butcher is my standard sea trout pattern. Cast diagonally upstream and brought back deep and slowly, the Butcher will often tempt sea trout which have been in the river system for several weeks, and these 'stale' sea trout are generally accepted to be the most difficult of all game fish to tempt with a fly. Fished singly, or better still in a team of two or three, the Butcher often brings fish to the bank when brighter flies are refused.

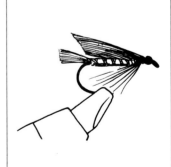

WINGED FLIES

Origin

This most famous of trout flies was first tied in 1854, at which time its inventors, Cannon William Greenwell and professional fly-tyer James Wright, used it as a general imitator of upwinged olives on the River Tweed. Apart from the addition of a tail to aid floating, the dry-fly dressing below is based on the original wet dressing.

Materials

Hook   Size 12 to 16 fine wire
Tying thread   Waxed yellow tying thread
Tail   Greenwell or furnace cock fibres
Body   Waxed yellow tying thread
Rib   Fine gold wire
Wing   Inside of a blackbird (or pale starling) wing
Hackle   Greenwell or Coch-y-bonddhu cock hackle
Head   Waxed yellow tying thread

Tying the Greenwell's Glory.

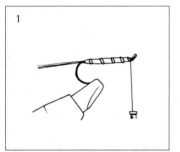

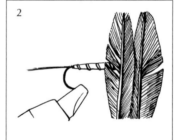

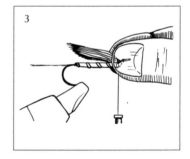

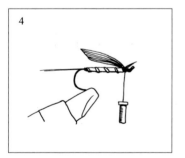

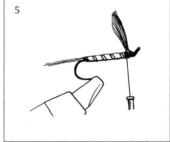

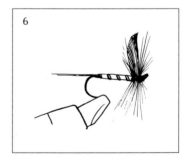

A Split-Winged Dry Fly –
Greenwell's Glory

Tying Hints

Step 1:   After tying the foundation layers, lock in the rib material and run the tying silk back to the head position to produce a neat slim body. Rib the body with an even spiral of the gold wire. With too much wire ribbing the fly will not float well, so space the ribs out – four or five turns are quite enough.

Step 2:   Now for the wings! Choose two matching wing feathers, one from each wing of the bird, and use your dubbing needle to select a pair of slips from the corresponding position on each feather.

Step 3:   Cut out the slips and place them with their shiny sides together. Align the tips precisely and position them over the hook so that the wing tips just reach the bend.

Step 4:   Without altering the position of the wing slips, change hands so that you can secure the wings using the pinch-and-loop technique. Make two more loops over the wings, pulling down tightly each time.

Step 5:   Trim off the excess wing material and lift the wings to the vertical position so that you can run the thread behind and underneath the wings; this will ensure the wings remain cocked upright.

Step 6:   Add the hackle in the usual way with two turns behind the wings and two more turns in front. Tie a neat head and secure it with a whip finish. Apply two coats of clear head varnish and the Greenwell's Glory is ready for action.

Variations on a Theme

The original Greenwell's Glory was tied with wings from the inside feathers of a blackbird wing and with soft coch-y-bonddhu hen hackles. The hackled Greenwell has no wings but is tied with two hackles – a furnace cock hackle is tied in first, leaving room for a medium-blue dun hackle in front.

Fishing Tips

The wet Greenwell is a good early season spate river fly whenever the water is reasonably clear. Used as a middle dropper or point fly it is also a fair imitation of the emerging Lake Olive.

Inevitably, such a successful pattern as the Greenwell's Glory led to many derivatives, both dry fly, wet fly and nymph. The Greenwell Nymph is a good imitation of the lighter olive nymphs. It has a thin abdomen, tied exactly as the body described above, a small thorax of grey fur, and a wing-case made of grouse hackles. The wing-case can be tied in exactly the same way as described for the Pheasant Tail Nymph. A sparse throat hackle of furnace cock adds the illusion of legs, but they should be kept very short.

It is as a dry fly that the Greenwell really excels, being in the opinion of many authoritative anglers, the best all-round imitator of the olives. It is only the most fastidious of fish that refuse a well-placed dry Greenwell when trout are feeding on olive duns.

WINGED FLIES _____

Origin

World-famous American fly fisher Lee Wulff devised a range of dry flies in the early 1930s. Today the Grey Wulff is one of the best known of all dry flies, catching trout wherever it is fished. To use animal hair in fly dressing was rather unorthodox sixty years ago, but the advantages of this durable material are now more widely appreciated.

Lee Wulff originally used the hair of an elk, but in the British Isles the Wulff flies are now most commonly tied with calf tail.

Materials

Hook   Sizes 8 to 14 fine wire
Tying thread   Black
Tail   Brown calf tail
Body   Grey rabbit fur
Wing   Brown calf tail
Hackle   Blue dun cock hackle
Head   Black tying thread

Tying Hints

Step 1:   Having wound a foundation layer take the tying thread back to the head position. Take a bunch of calf tail hair and lay it across the top of the hook so that it overlaps the eye by one hook gape. Use the pinch-and-loop method three times to lock the hair in place.

Step 2:   Pull the tips of the hair back towards the bend of the hook and wind six turns of tying thread close against the base of the hair to hold the wing upwards. Use the tying thread to divide the wings with a figure-of-eight whipping.

Step 3:   With sharp scissors, trim the waste material in a gentle taper to form an underbody to the fly. Take the tying thread behind the wings and down to the hook bend, covering the butt ends of the calf tail.

A Hair-Winged Dry Fly – Grey Wulff

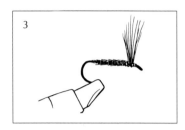

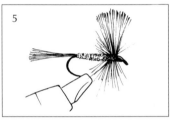

Tying the Grey Wulff.

Step 4: Tie in six to eight fibres of calf tail to make the tail. Dub rabbit fur on to the tying thread and wind the body of the fly.

Step 5: Tie in the blue dun cock hackle with two turns behind the wings and two turns in front. Make a neat, whip-finished head and apply two coats of head varnish.

Variations on a Theme

The Grey Wulff can be tied with squirrel tail instead of calf tail, and mole fur is sometimes substituted for rabbit as the body material. Instead of a dubbed body, grey wool is sometimes used.

Variants include the Grizzly, the Blonde, and the White Wulff, in which lighter materials are substituted for tail, body and wings.

Many anglers find the Royal Wulff a most attractive fly, and it seems the trout of fast rivers and streams are inclined to agree with them. The Royal Wulff differs from the other patterns in the series in that it has a body of peacock herl upon which is tied a band of red floss silk. The wings are white and the tail and hackle brown. White goat hair is an ideal material for the wings and tails of small versions of this fly.

WINGED FLIES

Origin

This series of lure flies originated in New Zealand, where the name comes from the bird whose feathers were used in the winging of the fly. The pattern described below is the Ace of Spades and was devised, as were so many of the Matuka variants now widely used in the British Isles, by the late David Collyer. Few experienced stillwater anglers would want to visit a rainbow trout fishery without having this pattern in their fly boxes.

Materials

Hook   Long shank sizes 6 to 10
Tying thread   Black
Body   Black chenille
Ribbing   Oval silver tinsel
Underwing   A crest of black hen hackle
Overwing   Dark bronze mallard
Throat hackle   Guinea fowl
Head   Black tying thread

Tying Hints

Fishing Tips

It is possible the Ace of Spades is taken as a fry imitation, for it certainly fishes well if retrieved erratically. In motion the brighter Badger Matuka is a realistic representation of a male stickleback in mating colours. As such it should be an excellent early season fly; but strangely on many waters this pattern remains effective through most of the season.

Step 1:   Start by taking the foundation layer back to the bend and tie in the tinsel ribbing and the chenille. Take the tying thread back to the head position and wind a body of chenille. Lock in the chenille at the head.

Step 2:   Next select two matching black hen hackles and remove the flue and fibres to leave a pair of wings about twice the length of the hook. Hold the wings on edge together with the shiny sides outwards. Remove all fibres from the bottom of the feathers up to the point where they overlap the bend of the hook. Tie the wing butts in securely just behind the eye of the hook.

Step 3:   Now for the tricky bit! Grip the tips of the wings firmly with your left hand, and use your right thumb and forefinger, to stroke vertically just those wing fibres which are above the shank of

A Matuka Fly – Ace of Spades

the hook. Keep the wing tensioned with your right hand as you make a securing turn with the ribbing, taking it over the wings and spiralling forward towards the head. Each time the rib passes over the wing take care to ease free any trapped wing fibres.

Step 4:   Once the ribbing is complete tie it off and add a beard hackle. Finally, tie in the mallard overwing and finish with a neat whip-finished head. Apply two coats of head varnish to complete the Ace of Spades.

Variations on a Theme

A popular version of this tying is the Badger Matuka which has a body of fluorescent orange wool and a pair of badger cock hackles as wings. Jungle cock cheeks are sometimes added to this already attractive lure.

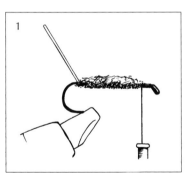
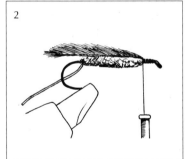
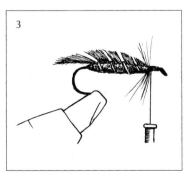
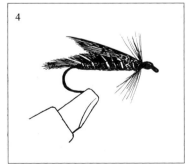

Tying the Ace of Spades.

MORE ADVANCED DRESSINGS ——————

Origin

The freshwater shrimp, *Gammarus pulex,* is found in most streams apart from those whose waters are very acidic. Shrimps also occur in several stillwaters, most notably spring-fed lakes with shallow gravelly margins. The tying below is from Derek Hoskin.

Materials

Hook   Size 12 to 14 forged
Tying thread   Olive
Underbody   Fine lead wire
Body   Olive seal's fur
Rib   Fine gold wire
Back   Polythene strip
Legs   Body fibres pricked out
Head   Olive tying thread

Fishing Tips

Shrimps swim in energetic bursts, surging up from the river bed and diving back just as quickly. This type of 'sink-and-draw' motion is easy to produce when you fish a weighted shrimp on a floating line. Cast the nymph and let it sink until you think it is at, or near, the bed of the river or lake. Now, as you retrieve line, the shrimp will rise up towards the surface. Cease bringing in line and the nymph will settle down again. A shrimp fished with six-inch pulls followed by two-second pauses can be very tantalizing to a trout, but if you should fail to get results try longer pulls at greater intervals so that the shrimp rises and falls further each time.

Tying Hints

Step 1:   Run the foundation thread part-way round the bend of the hook. Tie in the lead wire and run a double layer up to the head and back to the bend. Tie in the ribbing wire.

Step 2:   Cut a 2in strip of strong clear polythene about ⅛in wide and stretch it until its length increases to 3in. Tie the polythene in at its mid-point and fold both ends back over the hook bend. Dub on the seal's fur and wind a humped body, locking the thread at the head position.

Step 3:   Next pull the lower layer of polythene forward over the top of the hook and, keeping it under tension, lock it in at the head. Bring the ribbing forward in five or six evenly-spaced turns to create a segmented body. Tie in at the front and trim off the spare wire.

Step 4:   Now bring the other layer of polythene over the back of the shrimp and tie it in at the front. The body segments will show through the outer polythene in a most realistic manner. Add a small

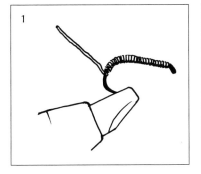
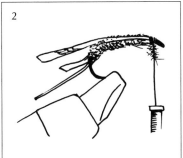
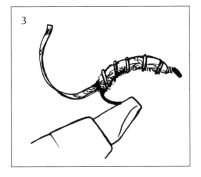
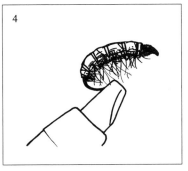

Tying a Shrimp.

head, whip-finish and apply two coats of head varnish. Finally, prick out fibres from the body material to represent the legs of the shrimp.

Variations on a Theme

Shrimps turn a pale orange colour during their mating season in summer. Then a mixture of olive and bright orange seal's fur makes a more realistic body representation.

Some fly tyers include a few feather fibres mixed in with the fur dubbing; these give more life-like legs when carefully pricked out under the body.

Heavily-weighted shrimps can be produced by binding layers of lead foil on to the top of the hook shank before dubbing on the body. In this way the humped back of the natural shrimp can be imitated. The subject of weighting is covered in more detail on pages 74-5.

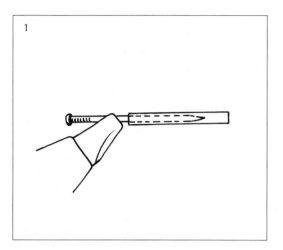

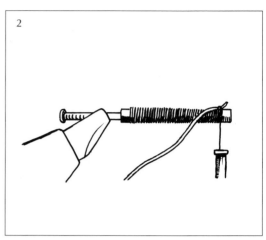

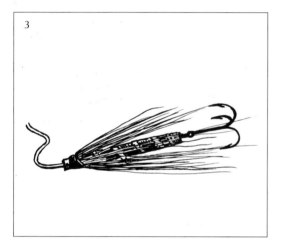

Tying a Tube Fly.

In the Beginning

Traditionally salmon flies, and to some extent also sea trout flies, have been difficult and time consuming to tie. It is not unusual for the list of materials required for the tying of a fully-dressed salmon fly to run to twelve or more items. Hair wing versions of these patterns are easier to tie and are often far more durable. Thankfully, the salmon seem no more reluctant to accept them than the more elaborate versions. It seems logical to carry this simplification to the extreme, and to use probably the most secure hooking device yet invented – the treble. The result is a range of tube flies which now account for as many if not more salmon each season than do the traditional single-hook prototypes.

Materials

Hook Trebles in sizes 8 to 12 for salmon, 10 to 14 for sea trout
Tying thread Black
Tubes Polythene or nylon for lightweight flies to be fished just

Tube Flies

beneath the surface on a floating line, or at line depth on a sinking line. Suitable plastic tubing is inexpensive, but empty tubes from ballpoint pens can also be brought into service after being cut to the required length. Aluminium or brass tubes can be used to make fast sinking flies, but they are more difficult to cast.

Bodies   Black floss
Rib   Silver tinsel
Wings   Black squirrel tail
Hackle   A black cock hackle can be added if required

Tying Hints

Step 1:   Cut the tube to the required length. Plastic tubes from ³/₄in to 2¹/₂in are most popular, but some sea trout anglers use tubes up to 4in long when fishing very deep water on dark nights.

Step 2:   Slide the tube over a nail of the right diameter, chosen so that it fits snugly inside the tube, and insert the nail into the jaws of the tying vice. Build a foundation layer of tying thread before winding on the body floss and ribbing it with tinsel. Start and finish the body ¹/₈in from each end of the tube.

Step 3:   The 'wings' of a tube fly often extend right around the tube, but on sea trout patterns I find it is better to place bunches of hair at four points around the tube so that the body and ribbing show through. The hair wing should extend beyond the end of the tube so that it partly obscures the treble hook. If you wish you can add a hackle at the front of the tube, but very few fly tyers bother with this refinement.

Variations on a Theme

Various colours of body floss can be used when tying a Tube Fly, and the wing can be made from hair of one colour or a mixture of various dyed hairs. Traditional hair winged patterns such as Sweeney Todd translate readily to the tube fly style of tying. The body floss is switched from black to magenta for the final third of the body length.

Fishing Tips

Thread the leader through the tube from head to tail before tying on the treble hook. On plastic tubes it is usually possible to push the treble shank part way into the tube. This greatly reduces the risk of the treble hook swinging round and catching on the leader during casting.

The flexibility of a plastic tube is an asset; it reduces leverage once a fish is hooked. For this reason metal tubes longer than 1¹/₂in are not recommended. Heavy tube flies are also dangerous when in the air, and it pays to wear head and eye protection in case something goes wrong during casting!

More Advanced Dressings —————

Why use Multi-Point Hooks?

Most fly patterns can be tied on double or treble hooks if you so wish. Indeed, many salmon and sea trout fishers are convinced that a small multi-point hook provides a much more secure hook hold than can be obtained with a single point hook. Occasionally, double and treble hooks are used simply because the extra metal in the hook adds weight to the fly and so allows deeper fishing with a floating line.

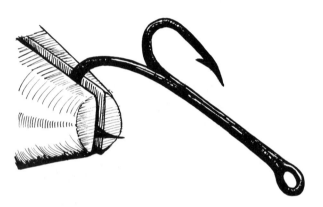

I suggest multi-point hooks should not be used when trout fishing, and particularly on rivers or lakes containing a significant proportion of undersized fish. It is much easier to release a trout which has been caught on a single hook. In fact the rules of most stillwater fisheries do not permit the use of double or treble hooks.

Wee Doubles

Fix the hook into the jaws of the vice, leaving the exposed point on the near side of the vice where you can more easily manoeuvre the thread and other materials around it. The fly should be tied with its wing positioned on the centre line of the hook and with the two points facing downwards.

If you find the unprotected hook point repeatedly snags your tying thread, fit a small piece of cork or plastic tubing over the point while you are tying.

Wee Doubles and Trebles

Trebles

Trebles are normally tied without a distinct wing, the material – usually hair – being spread more or less evenly around the hook. Many fly tyers don't bother to incorporate any body material; they simply wind a short foundation layer and tie winging material directly onto this.

Trebles are made by brazing a single eye-less hook onto the top of a double hook. So, if you do want to tie a feather-winged fly, then fit the wing directly above the single hook. This will ensure that the fly is well-balanced and swims on an even keel.

Fishing Tips

In summer, salmon often move to a fly very tentatively, and will turn away from anything they consider too large. Flies tied on size 12 or even 14 double hooks will sometimes do the trick. Dull patterns are often best when the water is low and clear.

Summer sea trout are notorious for slipping the hook as they leap and splash acrobatically on the surface. With small doubles or trebles and the fly tied directly onto the hook shank, I find that a higher proportion of hooked fish get landed.

More Advanced Dressings _____

What are the Advantages of Detached Body Flies?

You need quite a large hook if you want to tie a full-sized Mayfly or Daddy-Long-Legs body along the shank. A smaller and less conspicuous hook can be used if the body of the fly is extended beyond the bend of the hook or if the body is tied to the hook just at the head. There are other reasons though for choosing the detached body style. For example, you can make bodies from buoyant plastic materials such as short lengths of floating fly line which could not easily be threaded on to the shank of a hook.

Extended Bodies

Very long-bodied flies – for example, Damselflies – can be tied with their bodies extending beyond the bend of the hook. Deer hair is an ideal material for this type of body. It is easier to tie the body on a needle and connect it to the hook afterwards.

Step 1: Fix a fine strong needle into the jaws of the tying vice and run on a foundation of waxed thread. If a tail is required, tie this in, and tie in any ribbing material (unless the body is to be ribbed with tying thread).

Step 2: Remove a small bunch of deer fibres from a deer skin and catch the tips in at the tail position, with the butts pointing *away* from the fly body. If you have tied in ribbing material then run the thread to the other end of the body; otherwise leave it at the tail position.

Step 3: Pull the deer hair forward neatly and evenly over the foundation layer – be careful not to take the ribbing material with it – and hold it there with the tying thread while you rib the body. Tie off the ribbing and secure the front of the body with a whip finish.

Step 4: Slide the body gently off the needle and trim off the butts of the deer hair at a taper. Offer this taper up to the bend of the hook and tie it in. Add wings, thorax, hackles and head to complete the fly.

Flies with Extended and Detached Bodies

Detached Bodies

It is quite possible to tie a fly without the hook forming part of the body at all. The body may be tied from hair, as above, or it could be made by ribbing a piece of plastic tubing. Insulation stripped from telephone cable is useful as it comes in various colours, including ready ribbed!

The body can be attached right behind the eye of the hook. Cut the body material to a steep taper and whip this securely on top of the hook just behind the eye. Pull the body away from the hook at right angles and wind four tight turns of tying thread hard up against the body to hold it in that position. A hackle can now be spun onto the body material to complete the tying.

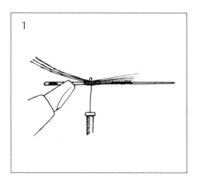

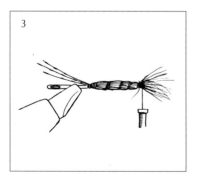

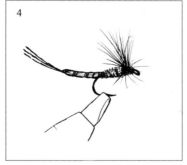

Tying an extended body fly.

MORE ADVANCED DRESSINGS ⎯⎯⎯⎯

Origin

Heavily weighted lures have long been recognized as effective takers of non-rising river trout. Indeed, many a wild old brown trout has fallen to a lead-head lure fished 'sink-and-draw' style. In recent times, with the growth in stillwater angling, large rainbow trout have also shown themselves to be vulnerable to lures weighted at the head and fished with a jerky retrieve.

Tying a lead-head lure.

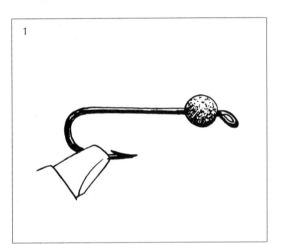

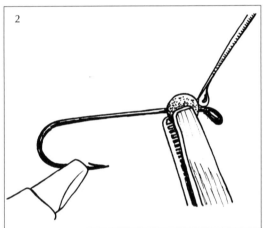

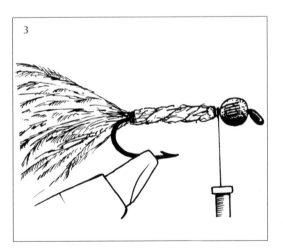

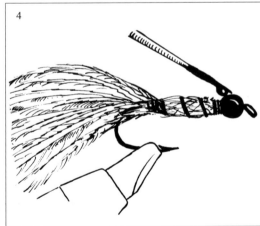

Lead-heads and Bead-Chain Lures

The most famous lead-head lure is the Dog Nobbler. Now a patented pattern, the design of this fly is credited to Trevor Housby. Other lead-heads have also been devised, many of them having chenille bodies with marabou wings and tails of various colours. The pattern described below is most effective in spring and autumn when the fish are lying deep.

Materials

Hook   Size 8 long shank
Tying thread   Black
Body   Yellow chenille
Rib   Silver tinsel
Tail   Red marabou
Wing   Black marabou
Head   Size BB shot with a deep central split

Tying Hints

Step 1:   Fix a long shank hook in the tying vice and loosely pinch on a weighting shot close against the eye and with the hook shank running through the centre of the shot. As lead is no longer permitted (a conservation measure aimed at protecting swans) use one of the modern lead-substitute alloy shots.

Step 2:   Put a drop of Superglue in the slot before closing it firmly with pliers. This will ensure that the shot remains in place.

Step 3:   Wind a foundation layer and then tie in a small pinch of red marabou fibre at the tail. Lock in the body material and ribbing. Run the thread back to just behind the shot and wind on the chenille body. Rib the body in the normal way and trim.

Step 4:   Tear off a tuft of black marabou and hold it above the hook so that the fibres extend half-way along the tail. Tie in the marabou wing using the pinch-and-loop method. Trim off the excess and whip-finish neatly behind the split shot. Apply two coats of varnish to both the whip finish and the split shot.

Bead-Chain Eyes

Bead chains of hollow metal balls can be cut into pairs and tied in at the front of a lure to represent eyes. The metal is not as dense as that used in split shot, so these types of lures are not quite as front heavy as lead-heads.

The lure pattern described above can be tied with bead-chain eyes. The tying sequence is as follows:

Step 1: Tie a foundation layer of waxed thread from the bend of the hook to the eye. Snip off two connected beads from the chain and hold them underneath the hook just behind the eye. Bind the beads to the hook using several turns of thread in a figure-of-eight tying. Run the thread back down the hook shank ready to tie in the tail and body materials.

Step 2: Secure the bead-chains with a touch of Superglue and leave to dry. Tie the remainder of the fly as detailed above. The beads can be left silver or, if you prefer, coated with black varnish when you seal the whip finish.

Tandem Lures

Several popular patterns can have flying treble hooks. Two examples are Loch Ordie, an excellent dapping fly, and Secret Weapon, a sea trout pattern devised by Hugh Falkus.

Step 1: Wind a foundation layer of tying thread from bend to eye of the treble. Thread a length of 25lb nylon monofilament through the eye and down the shank to leave an inch protruding beyond the end of the treble. Wind the tying thread tightly along the shank in close turns right back to the bend, trapping the nylon.

Step 2: Now carry the nylon around the bend of one of the hooks and pull it firmly towards the eye so that it is trapped in the gap between the hooks. Wind tight turns of tying thread along the shank, trapping the nylon again. Trim off the spare nylon and make a whip finish just behind the eye of the hook. If required, dress body material on to the treble.

Step 3: Align the flying treble below the main hook so that its eye is about one hook gape behind the bend of the main hook. Now continue to tie in the body, wing and hackle materials on to the main hook.

Once a fish is hooked, the shank of the hook acts as a lever, straining the hook hold each time the direction of pull changes. So, when a powerful fish surges up and down a pool, one minute pulling away from the angler and the next rushing towards him, it is not uncommon for the hook to fracture or to pull free. To reduce this problem, many popular sea trout flies are more often tied as tandem lures rather than singles. Tandems allow a large and highly visible fly to be presented to the quarry without the problem of excessive leverage once the fish is hooked. The two stages of a tandem fly are joined together as follows:

Step 1: Make a foundation layer on the rear hook by running tying thread from the bend to the eye. Thread a length of 20lb nylon monofilament through the eye of the hook and bind it along the hook shank.

Step 2: Return the nylon from bend to eye, thread it back through the eye and run the silk back from bend to eye, tying down the nylon. Body, wing and hackle materials can now be tied on to the rear hook.

Step 3: Fix the front hook in the vice and run foundation thread from the eye to the tail position. Hold the rear hook in position – half a hook length is the right separation for most patterns – and bind the two strands of nylon down with three turns of the tying thread. Adjust the positions carefully so that both hooks are held vertical before binding the nylon down with tight touching turns of tying thread along the hook shank to the head position.

Step 4: Pull back the loose ends of nylon along the sides of the front hook and return the tying thread in tight, close turns two-thirds of the way along the hook shank. Trim off the excess nylon and secure the tying thread with a whip finish. You are now ready to tie in the body, wing and hackle materials on the front hook.

Tandem Lures and FlyingTrebles

Tying a tandem lure.

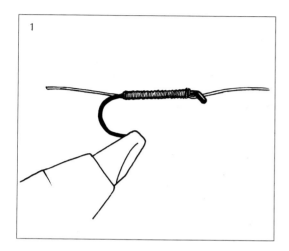

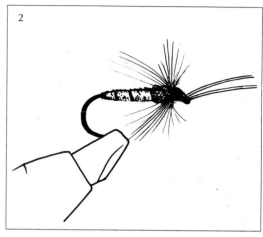

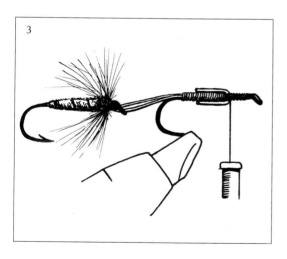

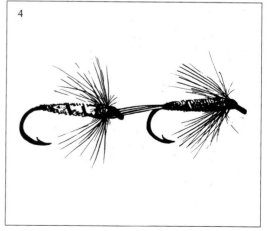

Special Techniques

Why Weight?

Trout get most of their food at or near the bed of the river or lake. And, in flowing water in particular, the fish soon learn that they can save a lot of unnecessary effort by holding station near the bed where the current is weakest. Only when a substantial supply of food is hatching or falling onto the water will trout lie just under the surface.

I am equally convinced that most of the time we tend to fish for salmon and sea trout with flies that do not swim deep enough to be fully effective. Indeed, if you know that the fish are there but you are getting no response, I think it is good advice in general to work your flies deeper rather than shallower.

There are several methods of weighting a fly, apart from the split shot method described earlier.

Lead Wire

This is one of the easiest materials to use provided your wire is of a fine gauge. Always wind the lead wire onto a bed of tying thread, never onto the bare hook shank.

Finally, give the lead a smear of varnish before running the tying thread along the weighted section of the shank and back again to the bend.

Copper Wire

A humped thorax of copper wire can be wound onto the hook before tying a nymph pattern. Again, run a foundation of tying thread along the shank before winding on the wire. Frank Sawyer used to tie his Pheasant Tail Nymphs without tying thread; he used just the wire and pheasant feather fibres.

Weighting with lead or copper wire.

Oliver Kite went a step further, tying his Bare Hook Nymph with nothing more than copper wire. Kite believed that nymph behaviour was of far more importance than shape or colour. Indeed, if there is no wing-case in your nymph design then it doesn't really matter if your tying comes loose and rotates on the hook, as long as it doesn't slide too far round the bend.

— Weighting Wet Flies and Nymphs

Lead Foil

A bulky wire body reduces the hooking potential of a fly. To avoid this problem lead foil can be added to the hook to create a hump away from the gape. Foil is also useful when you want to tie flat-bodied nymphs such as those of the March Brown or the Autumn Dun.

Cut one or more lead strips, the first slightly wider than the hook wire, and successive layers a little wider still. Tie on a foundation layer of waxed thread from eye to bend. Then, with the first strip of foil on top of the hook shank, return the thread in tight spiral turns back to the eye. Trim the next piece of lead a little shorter than the first and bind it in position in the same way. Continue to build up layers until you have the underbody shape and weight you require.

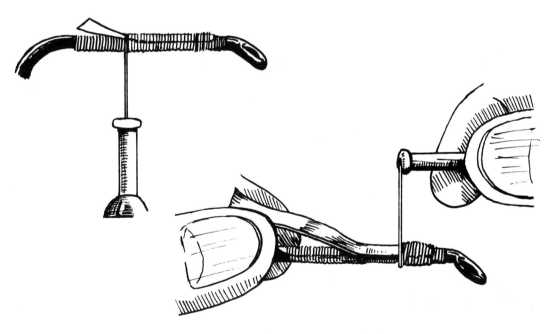

As an alternative, a single strip can be used. Cut it in a gradual taper and, once you have covered the shank in one direction, simply fold over the lead and continue the binding in the other direction.

Using lead foil.

75

SPECIAL TECHNIQUES _____

Properties of Deer Hair

The hair from the body of a deer has hollow fibres. It is strong, it springs back into place when bent, and it has a naturally oily finish which repels water. All this makes deer hair an excellent material for the tying of fly bodies, especially for flies which you want to float in choppy conditions.

Spinning a Deer Hair Body

Step 1: Prepare the foundation layer, running the thread from eye to bend. Tie in any tail material.

Step 2: Cut a bunch of deer hair away from the skin and hold it at the mid point. Shake out the short under-fur fibres. Hold the bunch by the roots and trim off the tips until the fibres are two-thirds of their original length.

Step 3: Place the deer hair on top of the hook at the tail position and take the tying thread over the bunch and back underneath the hook in a complete turn. Whilst loosely gripping the bunch of deer fibres, pull down lightly on the tying thread. Release the tension on the thread slightly and then tension it again. The hair will spin all around the shank of the hook. Ease the hair around the hook evenly, tighten the tying thread and wind another turn of thread just in front of the first.

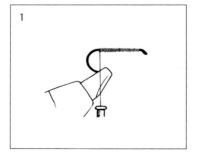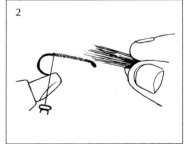

Spinning a deer-hair body.

Working with Deer Hair

Step 4:   Pull all the deer fibres towards the tail of the fly and wind two turns of tying thread hard against the deer hair to keep it folded back. Prepare another bunch of fibres and spin them onto the hook as close to the first bunch as possible. Tie in further bunches until you reach the head position.

Step 5:   Trim the deer hair to shape. To do this you will need sharp scissors, and you may well find it easier to hold the bend of the hook between finger and thumb rather than leave it in the vice. Wings and hackle can be added at this stage if required.

   Cut in the shape of a pitched roof, and with the addition of a throat hackle and a pair of antennae, the deer hair body is the basis of a superb sedge imitation. Bunches of fibres of various shades can be alternated to create a most realistic mottled effect. With a slip of green or orange wool (or dubbed seal's fur if you prefer) as an underbody or thorax, this is the basis of the renowned G&H sedge pattern.

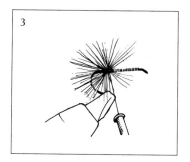

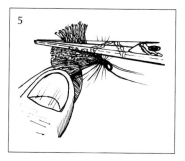

SPECIAL TECHNIQUES ──────────

Origin

Suspender patterns were first described by an American, Charles Brooks, and further developed by John Goddard and Brian Clarke to imitate mayfly nymphs and hatching sedge pupae. The idea is that the nymph can be made to hang just beneath the surface where it is most easily seen by a cruising trout.

Suspender flies.

The material used to obtain buoyancy is expanded polystyrene – ethafoam is equally suitable – in the form of small spheres. A single sphere is used in most suspender nymph patterns, but a pair can be used to represent bulging eyes. There is a lot to be said for exaggerating any prominent features of a fly when tying a matching artificial, and the Booby nymphs, with their huge polystyrene eyes, are a fine example of this practice.

Tying the Suspender Buzzer

Step 1: Wind a foundation layer of tying thread from the eye of the hook to a position well round the bend, as is usual for Buzzer imitations. Tie in a short tail of white hackle fibres and then the floss body material of black, red, green or brown, according to the species of Buzzer you want to copy. Tie in a length of thin silver wire, and then take the tying thread back to the thorax position.

Step 2: Wind on the body floss and rib it with the silver wire, locking both materials in at the thorax position. Now tie in a length of peacock herl and wind a humped thorax. Lock in and cut off the spare herl.

Suspender Flies

Step 3: Now for the suspender head. Take a single sphere of polystyrene and wrap it in a piece of nylon stocking. Stretch the stocking tight over the sphere and tie it onto the top of the hook shank at the head position. Whip-finish and varnish the thread behind the eye of the hook.

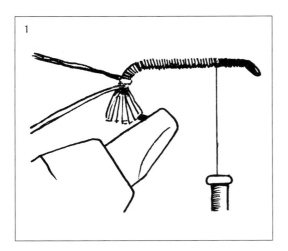

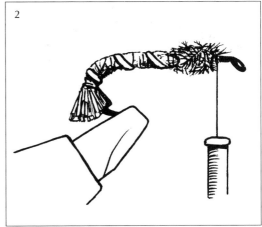

Tying a Suspender Buzzer.

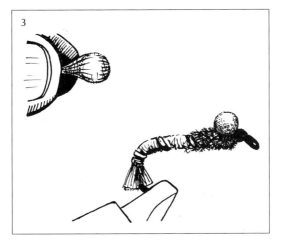

SPECIAL TECHNIQUES ─────────────

Origin

Imitations of the crane-flies are as old as fly fishing itself. These ungainly insects are amongst the least competent of pilots, crash-landing whenever the wind rises above a gentle breeze. Of the three hundred or so species of crane-flies native to the British Isles, only a tiny minority, mainly of the smaller species, are aquatic. But casualties occur increasingly amongst the terrestrial 'Daddies' as the season advances, and during August and September these welcome supplements to the trout diet are plentiful on most stillwaters and rivers bounded by meadowland.

The pattern described below was devised by Richard Walker.

Materials

Hook   Sizes 8 to 14 fine wire
Tying thread   Brown
Body   Pale cinnamon turkey fibres
Wings   Badger cock hackle tips
Legs   Cock pheasant tail fibres
Hackle   Pale ginger grizzle cock hackle

Tying Hints

Step 1:   Crane-flies do not have tails, so once you have prepared the foundation layer simply tie in the body fibres and wind a neat tapering body. Tie in a pair of grizzle cock hackle tips as wings, setting them slanting backwards over the body.

Step 2:   The next task is to provide the fly with some legs. These are made by knotting pheasant tail fibres to represent knee and ankle joints. Even though all insects have six legs, Richard Walker suggested eight legs be used. This was not because he thought the crane-fly was a flying spider, but because in time one or two would get bro!:en off. Anyway, thank goodness trout *don't* count the legs before deciding if an insect is genuine, or our hackled Mayflies would certainly not pass muster!

Fishing Tips

Crane-flies are attractive to trout throughout the season. In spring and early summer, try fishing miniature Daddies on size 14 hooks whenever a gusting wind brings a few of these flies to grief. I find this fly useful during the dog-days of summer as it often brings up a nice trout or two on rivers and streams when there is no sign of a hatch or fall of aquatic flies.

The larger versions are autumn patterns, and they account for some mighty rainbow trout towards the end of the season. In a flat calm you will probably find it best to cast the Daddy on to the water and leave it absolutely still; but whenever a breeze brings a bit of a ripple on to the surface it pays to draw this fly slowly through the surface creating a steady wake. The takes are often explosive, but it is not unusual for a trout to fail to engulf this large fly at the first attempt, so wait a second or more until the leader is drawn downwards before tightening.

Daddy-Long-Legs

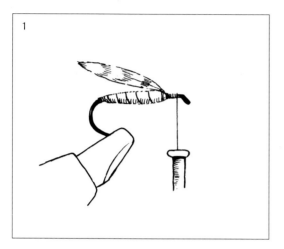

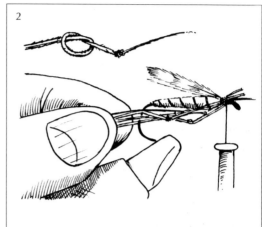

Step 3: The final step is to add four turns of ginger grizzle cock hackle, two behind the wings and two more in front, and to tie a neat head, whip-finish and varnish as usual.

Variations on a Theme

The pattern described above is a superb imitation of the cranefly, but its legs do tend to fracture with repeated casting. Geoff Bucknall ties a more durable version using strong brown nylon monofilament, knotted at suitable intervals, to represent the legs.

As a refinement, try including a nylon monofilament ribbing on the body. Brown Maxima gives a subtle ribbing effect, while a clear brand such as Kroic produces the effect of well-defined body segments.

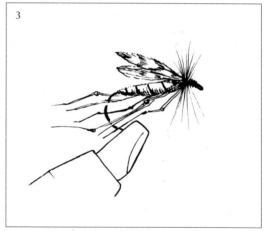

Tying a Daddy-Long-Legs.

Special Techniques

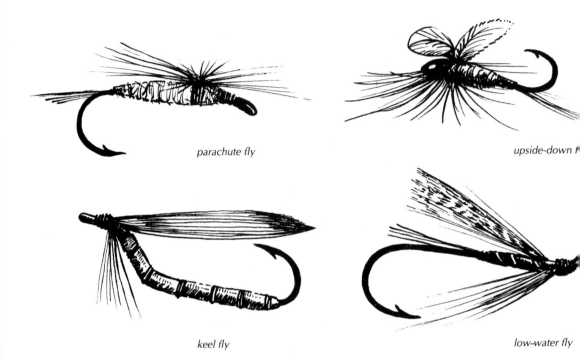

parachute fly

upside-down f

keel fly

low-water fly

Creative Solutions to Fishing Problems

From time to time a new style of hook or a special tying is devised in an attempt to solve a particular fishing problem. Some of these innovations rise quickly to prominence but are as quickly discredited and forgotten. Others are of genuine value and stand the test of time; a few of these are briefly discussed below.

Parachute Flies

William Bush, an American, devised and patented the parachute method of fly tying in 1933. The hackle is tied mid-way between eye and bend, and in the horizontal plane so that the fly drifts down gently onto the surface. Parachute flies sit in, rather than on, the surface, and so they are most often used as imitations of emerging duns or spent spinners.

Special Purpose Flies

It is possible to tie the hackle around a loop of its own stalk, by first fixing the stalk in a vertical position. Another method is to tie on to the hook a vertical post of deer hair or a loop of wire around which the hackle is wound.

Upside-Down Flies

To imitate a fly which sits on its legs with all of its body above the surface, John Goddard and Brian Clarke produced the upside-down (USD) Paradun range of flies. This type of fly sits on its hackles with the hook point in the air. Both from above *and below* the surface, the USD Paradun is a most realistic representation of an upwinged fly.

Keel Flies

There are problems to be overcome beneath the surface, too. Keel hooks are used to make flies which swim through the water with their points upwards; they are less likely to catch up in weed and other obstructions. The Dyffryn Demon, a sea trout keel pattern, probably owes much of its success to its ability to avoid snags while working deep where the larger sea trout lie.

When weighting these types of flies, it is very important to ensure that the lead foil is laid *beneath* the keel when the point is uppermost.

Low-Water Flies

In heavy or coloured water, salmon will seize a large fly, whereas they are more easily tempted with smaller flies when the water is low and warm. Smaller versions of traditional high water dressings can be tied on large strong hooks, although there are also many excellent summer patterns which are only ever tied as low-water flies.

Sea trout flies can also be tied in this manner, and they can be quite effective for fish which merely nip at the tail of a fully-dressed version without engulfing the hook.

Special Techniques _____

Pens

Pens intended for drawing on overhead transparencies are ideal for colouring both hair and feathers. There are two basic types – waterproof and washable. Obviously you need the waterproof ones.

You can dye materials darker but not lighter using pens; so start with pale feathers and fur, or bleach them white first. (It is important to rinse and dry materials thoroughly after bleaching them.)

Spun deer hair bodies can be trimmed into almost any ·shape if you have the patience. The hollow tips of the fibre can then be coloured by gently stroking them with the tip of the pen. Apply the lighter tones first and then add fine detail in darker colours.

Paint

Cellulose varnish or lacquer is available in a range of colours, and allow you to make flies with neat strong heads. The more elaborate lure patterns can be produced with multi-colour heads and eyes. Cellulose paint, as used in model making, is available in tiny pots. It will adhere to any reasonably firm surface, such as a split shot head, a hook shank or even a feather.

A most effective eyed lead-head can be produced as follows:

Step 1: Having first completed the tying of the fly, give the whole of the split shot a coat of black paint and allow it to dry.

Step 2: Pick up a blob of white paint on the end of a needle and touch it on to the side of the shot. A circle of paint will transfer to the shot. Pick up another blob of white paint, the same size as the first, and transfer a circle to the other side of the shot. Clean the needle and again wait until the paint dries.

Step 3: Pick up a smaller blob, this time of red paint, and transfer it to the centre of one of the white eyes. Repeat for the other eye, clean the needle and allow the paint to dry.

Fly with artificial Jungle Cock cheeks.

Step 4: Finally, add a tiny spot of black paint within, but to the front or rear of, the red spot. In this way you can produce an eye which appears to be looking either forwards or backwards.

84

Using Pens and Paints

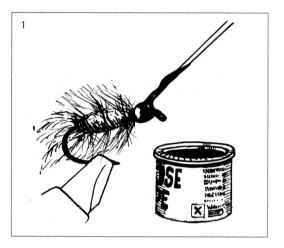

Artificial Jungle Cock Feathers

The Jungle Cock is now bred in captivity and its feathers can be purchased legitimately; but if you have none, and are tying a pattern which calls for 'Jungle Cock cheeks', you can use a plain feather and add spots of white and yellow paint to represent the eyed feather.

Useful Information

Wet Flies

Teal, Blue and Silver

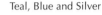

Teal, Blue and Silver

Hook   6 to 14 forged
Tying thread   Black
Tail   Golden pheasant tippets
Body   Flat silver tinsel
Ribbing   Fine silver wire
Wing   Barred teal breast feather
Hackle   Bright blue cock
Head   Black tying thread
Tying Hints   Pages 56-7

Tying Hints   Pages 56-7

Mallard and Claret

Mallard and Claret

Hook   10 to 14 forged
Tying thread   Black
Tail   Golden pheasant tippets
Body   Claret seal's fur
Ribbing   Fine gold wire
Wing   Brown mallard
Hackle   Natural red cock
Head   Black tying thread
Tying hints   Pages 40-1, 56-7

Iron Blue Dun

Iron Blue Dun

Hook   14 to 16 forged
Tying thread   Claret
Tail   White hackle fibres
Body   Mole fur
Hackle   Dark blue dun cock
Head   Claret tying thread
Tying hints   Pages 40-1, 56-7

Fly Tying from Menus

There are some excellent books, intended for the fly tyer, which do not explain tying techniques; instead they give tying menus plus a diagram or photograph of the finished fly. The details below are in just that form, but I have also included page references to tying techniques and similar fly patterns described earlier in this book. With this information you should be able to work through any of the patterns listed. This will be good preparation for tying other fly patterns from just a tying list and diagram.

Twelve Popular Trout Patterns

Snipe and Purple

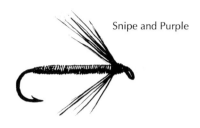
Snipe and Purple

Hook   12 to 16 forged
Tying thread   Purple
Body   Purple tying thread
Hackle   Dark snipe hackle
Head   Purple tying thread
Tying hints   Pages 31–3

March Brown

March Brown

Hook   12 or 14 forged
Tying thread   Brown
Tail   Patridge back feather fibres
Body   Brown wool
Ribbing   Fine gold wire
Hackle   Brown partridge back feather
Head   Brown tying thread
Tying hints   Pages 33   4

Dry Flies

Coachman

Coachman

Hook   12 to 16 fine wire
Tying thread   Black
Body   Bronze peacock herl
Wings   White duck
Hackle   Natural red cock
Head   Black tying thread
Tying hints   Pages 40, 50–1

USEFUL INFORMATION

Kite's Imperial

Kite's Imperial (Oliver Kite)

Hook   14 to 16 fine wire
Tying thread   Purple
Tail   Honey dun hackle fibres
Body   Natural heron herl
Ribbing   Fine gold wire
Thorax   Natural heron herl
Hackle   Honey dun cock
Head   Purple tying thread
Tying hints   Pages 40-1

Damselfly

Damselfly (Thomas Clegg)

Hook   12 long shank
Tying thread   Black
Body   Detached body made from a length of dyed-blue floating fly line
Ribbing   Black thread along the whole of the body
Wings   Four cock hackle points tied in two groups sloping backwards in 'V' formation
Hackle   Slate blue and dark brown hackles wound together
Head   Black tying thread
Tying hints   Pages 70-1, 82-3

Rat-Faced MacDougall

Rat-Faced MacDougall (Harry Darbee)

Hook   10 to 14 fine wire
Tying thread   White
Tail   Dark ginger hackle fibres
Body   Light tan deer hair spun and clipped
Wings   Cree grizzle hackle tips
Hackle   Dark ginger cock
Head   White tying thread
Tying hints   Pages 78-9

Twelve Popular Trout Patterns

Lures

Jersey Herd (Tom Ivens)

Hook   8 to 10 long shank
Tying thread   Black
Tail   Three strands of peacock herl
Underbody   Floss silk
Overbody   Flat copper tinsel
Back   Bronze peacock herl
Hackle   Hot orange
Head   Bronze peacock herl
Tying hints   Pages 48-9

Jersey Herd

Viva

Hook   6 to 10 long shank
Tying thread   Black
Tail   Green fluorescent wool
Body   Black chenille
Ribbing   Flat silver tinsel
Wings   Black marabou plume
Throat hackle   Black cock hackle fibres
Head   Black tying thread
Tying hints   Pages 72-3

Viva

Appetiser (Bob Church)

Hook   6 to 10 long shank
Tying thread   Black
Tail   Mixed orange, green and silver mallard fibres
Body   White chenille
Ribbing   Oval silver tinsel
Underwing   White marabou plume
Overwing   Grey squirrel
Hackle   Mixed orange, green and silver mallard fibres
Head   Black tying thread
Tying hints   Pages 62-3, 72-3

Appetiser

USEFUL INFORMATION

Fly Tying and Game Angling Organizations

The Fly Dressers Guild
The Guild has some fifty branches throughout the British Isles where members meet to exchange ideas and to hear from noted experts on aspects of fly tying and fly fishing.
Membership Secretary: Errol A. Walling, 29 Windmill Hill, Ruislip, Middlesex HA4 8PY.

Salmon and Trout Association (S&TA)
The S&TA coordinates game angling interests and organizes competitive fly fishing in England at national and international level.
S&TA, Fishmongers' Hall, London Bridge, London EC4R 9EL.
Tel: 071 283 5838.

National Anglers Council (NAC)
The NAC, in conjunction with the S&TA and the Fly Dressers Guild, arranges examinations for candidates who wish to become qualified instructors in game angling. Fly tying is an optional element of the NAC qualification. Mr Peter Tombleson (Executive Director), 11 Cowgate, Peterborough PE1 1LZ. Tel: 0733 54084.

Scottish Anglers National Assembly (SANA)
SANA coordinates game angling in Scotland. Mr Mike Shanks (Hon. Secretary), Craiganrioch, Kilkerran Road, Campbelltown, Argyll PA28 6JN. Tel: 0586 54343.

Welsh Salmon & Trout Angling Association (WSTAA)
WSTAA is the co-ordinating body for game angling in Wales, and organizes competition angling at national and international level. Would-be angling instructors may gain a WSTAA coaching qualification by taking the WSTAA coaching examination. Mr Moc Morgan (Hon. Secretary), Swyn Teifi, Pontrhydfendigaid, Ystrad Meurin, Dyfed SY25 6BB. Tel: 09745 316.

The Anglers' Co-operative Association (ACA)
The ACA is a pollution fighting body with the interests of all anglers at heart. The address for correspondence is 23 Castlegate, Grantham, Lincs NG31 6SW. Tel: 0746 61008.

Addresses

Fly Tying Tuition

Many local education authorities provide evening classes in fly tying. Classes usually start in September. These are popular and often over-subscribed, so early application is advisable. In addition, most good fly fishing schools include an element of fly tying in their tuition, and some run courses devoted solely to fly tying. Two of these are listed below:

West of England Centre of Game Angling
Caynton House, Torrington, Devon EX38 8AL. Tel: 0803 23256.

West Wales School of Flyfishing
Ffoshelyg, Lancych, Boncath, Dyfed SA37 0LJ. Tel: 023977 678.

Publications

Flydresser
The Fly Dressers Guild publishes a quarterly magazine, *Flydresser,* containing news, reviews and tying information. *Flydresser* is issued free to members. Editorial/contributions to Mr A Deacon, Editor, *Flydresser,* 1 Ferndale Cottages, Osmers Hill, Wadhurst, East Sussex TN5 6QJ. Tel: 089288 2153.

Below are some of the top game angling publications which are a valuable source of information. Editors are always on the look out for articles on new materials, techniques or fly patterns.

Trout and Salmon
Editor: Sandy Leventon, Bretton Court, Peterborough PE3 8DZ. Tel: 0733 264666.

Trout Fisherman
Editor: Chris Dawn, Bretton Court, Peterborough PE3 8DZ. Tel: 0733 264666.

Practical Gamefishing
Editor: John Wilshaw, 118 Manor Way, Deeping St James, Nr. Peterborough PE6 8PY. Tel: 0778 342848.

ADDRESSES

Salmon Trout & Sea-Trout
Editor: David Goodchild, Gamefishing Publications Ltd, The Lodge, Meridian House, Bakewell Road, Orton Southgate, Peterborough PE2 0XU. Tel: 0733 371937.

Fly Tying and Fly Fishing
Editor: Mark Bowler, Gamefishing Publications Ltd, The Lodge, Meridian House, Bakewell Road, Orton Southgate, Peterborough PE2 0XU. Tel: 0733 371937.

Suppliers of Hooks, Tools and Materials

Partridge of Redditch (Hook-makers)
Mount Pleasant, Redditch, West Midlands B97 4JE. Tel: 0527 43555.

Mustad (Hook-makers)
2 Brindley Road, Peterlee, Co. Durham SR8 2LT. Tel: 091 5869533.

Piscatoria (Fly-tying tools)
3a Hebden Court, Bakewell, Derbyshire. Tel: 062981 4770.

Tom Saville (Hooks, tools and materials)
Unit 17, Salisbury Square, Nottingham NG7 2AB.
Tel: 0602 784248.

Fishermen's Feathers
Hillend Farm, Station Road, Bransford, Worcestershire WR6 5JU.
Tel: 0905 830548.

Lureflash Products (Tools, hooks and materials)
10 Adwick Road, Mexborough, South Yorkshire S64 0AW.
Tel: 0709 580238.

Campbell Black & Co (Hooks, tools and materials)
Rood End House, 6 Stortford Road, Great Dunmow, Essex
CM6 1DA. Tel: 0371 873595.

Sussex Feathers
32a Sedlescombe Road South, Hastings, St Leonards-on-Sea, East Sussex TN38 0TB.

Glossary

Abdomen   The segmented rear section of an insect's body.

Badger hackle   A hackle having a black centre and white outer fibres, sometimes tipped with black.

Barb   The backward-facing projection cut into a hook near the point to reduce the chances of a hooked fish escaping. Barbless hooks have been shown to achieve similar results.

Bi-visible   A fly with both light and dark coloured hackles to give good visibility in both light and shaded water.

Blue Dun hackle   A slate-blue or grey hackle.

Bucktail   Deer tail. Also fry-imitating lures tied with deer hair wings.

Cape   The neck of poultry or game birds, from whence hackle feathers are obtained.

Chenille   A furry rope-like material used for lure bodies.

Coch-y-bonddhu hackle   A hackle with black centre and red edges tipped with black.

Cock hackles   The neck feathers of a cockerel.

Cree hackle   A barred black, red and ginger hackle, sometimes with cream or white flecks.

Detached body   Fly bodies tied not around the shank of the hook but attached only at the head of the fly.

Dry fly   A fly designed to float on the surface of the water.

Dubbing   The technique of spinning fur on to waxed thread and winding it around a hook shank to make a fly body.

Dun   The first winged stage of an upwinged insect.

Dun hackle   A greyish brown hackle.

Ethafoam   A synthetic material useful for making floating flies. (*See* suspender nymphs.)

Floss   Multi-strand silk or synthetic substitute used in fly bodies.

Fluorescent   Material which emits light of a visible colour when ultra-violet light falls upon it.

Furnace hackle   A hackle with black centre and red edges.

Golden Pheasant   Game bird whose crest, neck and wing feathers are used extensively in fly patterns.

Greenwell hackle   A hackle with red centre and ginger edges.

Grizzle hackle   Hackle with black and white bars (as Plymouth Rock).

Hackle   A neck feather tied to represent the legs of an insect.

Herl   The individual fibres of a feather, especially ostrich and peacock, used as tail and body materials.

GLOSSARY

Honey Dun hackle   A brown hackle with light ginger edges.

Ibis   Red feathers used as tails of flies. Substitutes include dyed swan and goose wing feathers.

Jungle cock   An Indian game bird whose hackles have distinctive cream 'eye' markings.

Lurex   A plastic material which is available in many colours including gold and silver, used as a substitute for tinsel.

Marabou   Turkey feather fibres used extensively as wings and tails of lures.

Mylar   Metallic plastic available in sheet or plaited tube form. The tubing can be used to simulate scales on the flanks of fry-imitating lures.

Palmer   A hackle wound spirally along the body of a fly.

Parachute fly   A fly with its hackle wound in the horizontal plane.

Plastazote   Buoyant plastic material similar to ethafoam.

Plymouth Rock hackle   A hackle with a grey centre and bands of black and white.

Polypropylene   Synthetic material available in very fine fibres suitable for dubbing or in coarser strands which can serve as wing or tail materials.

Polyvinyl chloride   PVC is an almost clear soft plastic used to create translucent bodies.

Spinner   The final adult stage of an upwinged insect.

Tandem lure   A lure consisting of two or more in-line hooks connected by short lengths of strong nylon.

Thorax   The front portion of the body of an insect to which the wings and legs are attached.

Tippet   A small orange and black barred feather from the golden pheasant.

Topping   A curved narrow gold feather from the crest of a golden pheasant.

Wet fly   An artificial fly designed to swim beneath the surface.

Whip finish   A knot use to secure the tying thread upon completion of the head of a fly.

Whisks   The individual filaments tied to represent the tails or *setae* of an insect

Wing-case   The humps containing the developing wings on the back of nymphs nearing maturity.

Further Reading

Fly-Tying

Dawes, M., *The Fly Tyer's Manual* (Collins, 1985)
Gathercole, P., *The Handbook of Fly Tying* (The Crowood Press, 1989)
Wakeford, J., *Flytying Techniques* (A & C Black, 1980)
Walker, R., *Fly Dressing Innovations* (A & C Black, 1974)

Fly Patterns

Price, T., *Fly Patterns – An International Guide* (Ward Lock, 1986)
Roberts, J., *A Guide to River Trout Flies* (The Crowood Press, 1989)
Roberts, J., *The New Illustrated Dictionary of Trout Flies* (Allen & Unwin, 1986)
Steward, T., *Two Hundred Popular Flies and How to Tie Them* (Benn, 1979)
Williams, A.C., *A Dictionary of Trout Flies* (A & C Black, 1949)

Trout Fly Identification

Goddard, J., *Trout Fly Recognition* (A & C Black, 1966)
Goddard, J., *Trout Flies of Stillwater* (A & C Black, 1975)
Harris, J. R., *An Angler's Entomology* (Collins, 1952)
Smith, R., *Life in Ponds and Streams in Britain* (Jarrold, 1979)

Fly Selection and Fishing Tactics

Church, B. & Gathercole, P., *Imitations of the Trout's World* (The Crowood Press, 1985)
Clarke, B. & Goddard, J., *The Trout and the Fly* (Benn, 1980)
O'Reilly, P., *Tactical Fly Fishing* (The Crowood Press, 1990)
Roberts, J., *To Rise a Trout* (The Crowood Press, 1988)
Sawyer, F., *Nymphs and the Trout* (A & C Black, 1974)

INDEX